THE REAL READER'S QUAR͏

Slightly Foxed

'Ring Out, Wild Bells'

NO.68   WINTER 2020

Editors Gail Pirkis & Hazel Wood
Marketing and publicity Stephanie Allen & Jennie Harrison Bunning
Bookshops Anna Kirk
Subscriptions Hattie Summers & Jess Dalby

Cover illustration: Coralie Bickford-Smith, 'Winter's Dance'

Coralie Bickford-Smith is one of the most renowned designers in the publishing industry, especially recognized and celebrated for her illustrated covers of Penguin's clothbound classics. Her first book, *The Fox and the Star*, was named Waterstones Book of the Year. Her third book, *The Song of the Tree*, is a lyrical, heart-warming new tale about a bird that loves to sing in the towering tree at the heart of the jungle. For more of her work visit www.cb-smith.com.

Design by Octavius Murray
Layout by Andrew Evans
Colophon and tailpiece by David Eccles

© The contributors 2020

Published by Slightly Foxed Limited
53 Hoxton Square
London N1 6PB

tel 020 7033 0258
email office@foxedquarterly.com
www.foxedquarterly.com

Slightly Foxed is published quarterly in early March, June, September and December

Annual subscription rates (4 issues)
UK and Ireland £48; Overseas £56

Single copies of this issue can be bought for £12.50 (UK) or £14.50 (Overseas)

All back issues in printed form are also available

ISBN 978-1-910898-49-9
ISSN 1742-5794

Printed and bound by Smith Settle, Yeadon, West Yorkshire

Contents

Contents

The Slightly Foxed Podcast

A new episode of our podcast is available on the 15th of every month. To listen, visit www.foxedquarterly.com/pod or search for Slightly Foxed on Audioboom, iTunes or your podcast app.

Subscriber Benefits

Slightly Foxed can obtain any books reviewed in this issue, whether new or second-hand. To enquire about a book, to access the digital edition of *Slightly Foxed* or to view a list of membership benefits, visit www.foxedquarterly.com/members or contact the office: 020 7033 0258/office@foxedquarterly.com.

From the Editors

After probably the strangest year that most of us have ever experienced, London is starting to feel more familiar. There are lighted office windows around Hoxton Square, and there's traffic again in Old Street, now including shoals of bikes, some darting in and out of the cars and vans like minnows, some wobbling dangerously. There are a lot of new and inexperienced bike riders in London these days, and whether you're walking or driving you have to look out. At *Slightly Foxed* the office is buzzing, and readers and contributors have been active too, putting pen to paper, or rather finger to key, to give the two of us plenty to read after lockdown. Sadly we had to cancel Readers' Day this year, but we've booked the Art Workers' Guild for 6 November 2021, and we look forward very much to seeing you there.

Despite everything and thanks to you, we've had a busy autumn. Roger Hudson's *An Englishman's Commonplace Book* has struck a note with many of you, perfect as a Christmas present or simply something to cheer yourselves up. A piquant mix of thoughts, contemporary accounts and observations from many different historical sources collected over forty years, it's amusing, surprising and thought-provoking.

The latest Slightly Foxed Cubs, recently out, are Rosemary Sutcliff's *Frontier Wolf* and *The Lantern Bearers*, the next two in her wonderful series of novels on the Roman occupation of Britain which carry on the story begun in *Eagle of the Ninth* and *The Silver Branch*, published last year. In 2021 we'll be adding the last three books in the sequence: *Dawn Wind* in March and *Sword Song* and *The Shield Ring* in September. Together these novels weave together fact and fiction to take young (and older) readers on an unforgettable journey through the fascinating and mysterious world of Roman Britain and what came after. There is nothing quite like them and they are flying off the shelves. All the titles can be ordered or pre-ordered now, so if you are keen to collect the whole series, do seize the moment while stocks last.

Our winter Slightly Foxed Edition is a book by another writer with an extraordinary ability to evoke the past, though in this case he's writing about his own childhood, Laurie Lee's *Cider with Rosie* (see p. 15). Lee grew up in the remote Cotswold village of Slad in the years during and after the First World War, in a large, warm, hugger-mugger family of seven with a mother who was an ever-optimistic dreamer of dreams who 'couldn't keep a neat house for her life'. Their father had abandoned them and times were hard, but despite the poverty and the undeniable harshness of rural life, for Laurie the valley was full of a wonder that suffuses this magical book. Definitely one for curling up with when it's cold outside – literally and meta-phorically.

And finally to keep the grey matter active do have a go at our annual literary Christmas crossword, which you'll find at the end of the cata-logue. Entries should be with us by 15 January 2021 and the first correct one drawn out of a hat will receive a free subscription. Meanwhile, a very special thank you for all your support. We both wish you the happiest possible Christmas and an optimistic New Year.

GAIL PIRKIS & HAZEL WOOD

John Watson

Ring Out, Wild Bells!

MARIANNE FISHER

Imagine you are walking in the English countryside and come to a village. As the day is hot and the church is open, you step inside to look around and rest in the predictably cool and dim interior. There are some things that the vast majority of church buildings in the British Isles seem to share: the 'odour of sanctity' (a combination of furniture polish, lilies and slightly damp stonework); the kneelers stitched by parishioners; a wall display or prayer tree made by the Sunday-school children; and a series of polite little notices – 'Please close the door. PIGEONS!!!'

And then there are the books. Each church has its Bible, obviously, stacks of hymn books ready to be handed out on Sundays, and aged copies of the *Book of Common Prayer*, these perhaps kept in a glass-fronted cabinet and used only by the few faithful who venture out for Evensong. All these you would expect to find as you wander around, your eyes gradually growing used to the shadows after the bright sunshine outside.

There is, however, another book. Behind a locked door, in an upper room, there is likely to be a slim quarto volume that you might not expect. You must be intrepid to reach it: you will need a key to unlock the door; you will need to climb a ladder or a spiral stair; there may be narrow passages through the thick walls, or boarded

---

Jasper Snowdon, *Diagrams* (1881, 14th ed., 2011)
Yorkshire Association of Change Ringers · Hb · 104pp · £12 ·
ISBN 9789956942807
To order visit www.yacr.org.uk/books

walkways through the roof-space, running over the top of the vaulted ceiling of the church below. Finally you will pass notices: 'No Entry!' 'Danger!' 'Don't Touch the Ropes!'

We have, of course, reached the ringing chamber, and the book we've been seeking is Jasper Snowdon's *Diagrams* (1881), published originally by the author and since 2011 by the Yorkshire Association of Change Ringers. It is now in its fourteenth edition, and there is a copy in just about every tower with bells, not only in England but also in Wales, Scotland, Ireland and anywhere else in the world where change ringing is practised: America, Canada, Australia, New Zealand . . . The art of change ringing – ringing bells in particular patterns rather than crashing them all together at once – was a peculiarly English innovation. The earliest references are from the eastern counties of England around the year 1600, but the landmark publication came in 1668 with Richard Duckworth and Fabian Stedman's co-written *Tintinnalogia*.

The technological breakthrough that allowed the Exercise, as change

HAND-STROKE   BACK-STROKE

ringing is known, to develop was the realization that bells could be hung on a large wheel so that the mouth of the bell can swing through a full 360 degrees. By using the rope to vary the energy in that swing, the skilled ringer can exercise very fine control over the tons of metal turning rhythmically above his or her head.

Each ringer operates one bell only (though some particularly fine ringers can handle two as a party piece), and the whole endeavour works by pairs of bells swapping places according to a predetermined sequence. Every bell must sound once before any of the others can sound again, and each time your bell sounds you can climb either one place down the order (for example, sounding third instead of fourth), or one place up (sounding fifth instead of fourth), or you can stay where you were.

Using these simple rules, many different sequences have been developed, all moving the bells from their starting point in 'rounds' (ringing down the scale from highest-pitched bell to lowest), through a set of changes, and back into rounds without any repetition. Each order of bells must appear only once, or else the ringing is deemed 'false'. As in a part-song such as 'London Bridge' or 'Frère Jacques', everyone follows the same path. The difference is that whereas in a part-song everyone starts at the beginning, each singer waiting his or her turn to come in, in ringing the bells all set off together – like Tube trains all departing different stations on the Circle Line at the same time.

There are literally thousands of these sequences, referred to as 'methods'. Some are very old, like Grandsire Triples, which was already well established around 1700; others are relatively new, like Rook and Gaskill, which dates from 2003. Indeed, people are still discovering and naming new methods today. Some methods are simple, such as the Plain Bob family; others are fiendishly complicated, like Orion Surprise Maximus. Change ringing is commonly practised on anything between four and sixteen bells – though six, eight, ten and twelve are the most usual numbers – and the duration can be anything from a few minutes' 'service touch' before worship, to a quarter peal (about 50 minutes), a peal (about 3½ hours), or an epic 'long length'. Some readers will be familiar with Dorothy L. Sayers's *The Nine Tailors* (1934), in which Lord Peter Wimsey participates in a 9-hour performance of Kent Treble Bob, but the current record dwarfs that not-inconsiderable achievement: 40,320 changes of Plain Bob Major, rung in 17 hours 58 minutes at the Loughborough Bell Foundry in 1963.

But let us return to *Diagrams*, as it is ubiquitous among ringers from the newest learners to the superstars pushing the boundaries of the Exercise. Jasper Snowdon was born in Ilkley, Yorkshire, in 1844. His father was a vicar, and Jasper probably learnt to handle a bell as a teenager. He became the first President of the Yorkshire Association of Change Ringers on the society's formation in 1876, and he wrote a number of respected books on ringing before his death from typhoid fever in 1885.

One of those books was *Standard Methods in the Art of Change Ringing*, which comprised two parts: the first, *Letterpress*, contains mostly textual description and has sunk into relative obscurity; the second, *Diagrams*, goes from strength to strength. *Diagrams* is a book not of words but of pictures. Or, more accurately, it is a book of lines, numbers and peculiar names. It contains a selection of the more commonly rung methods, showing the paths you need to learn in order to ring them. The treble (the smallest bell) follows a simple line, shown in red; the other bells 'do the work', which is marked in blue. The numbers in circles indicate where each bell starts when the conductor (the person in charge) says 'Go'. *Diagrams* also shows you what to do if the conductor calls 'Bob' or 'Single' – instructions that shuffle the bells around so that different rows (that is, orders of bells) can be reached, thus allowing the ringing to continue for longer without being false or coming back into rounds too soon.

My mother and my partner, who both learnt to ring before I did, have the 'old'

St Simon's Bob   Stedman

version of *Diagrams*, which is bound in red cloth. I have the 'new' one, which is bound in blue faux leather. Both bear the single word DIAGRAMS in gold capital letters across the front. Both versions start with Minimus methods (rung on four bells), then move on to Doubles (on five), Minor (six), Triples, Major, Caters, Royal, Cinques and, finally, Maximus (rung on twelve bells). My version contains more methods, but the old red one is more spaciously laid out and is printed on heavier, cream-coloured paper. I confess I prefer the old one, though my copy – inscribed from my mother for my birthday in 2014 – is dear to me nonetheless.

Most tower copies of *Diagrams* fall open at particularly well-used pages – Plain Bob Minor, Grandsire Triples, Yorkshire Major – but a personal copy carries more intimate traces. The earlier sections of mine are particularly heavily used. Some pages are marked with slips of paper or sticky notes, among them conventional methods such as Stedman Doubles, St Nicholas Doubles and London Surprise Major, but also some peculiarities – why did I mark Middlesex Bob Triples and Grandsire Minor, I wonder? Bristol Surprise Major is annotated with pencil B's and H's, traces of my working out which blows are at backstroke and which at hand. Grandsire Doubles, I notice, is besmirched with tomato sauce – I must have been poring over it as I ate dinner before going out to an evening practice. Plain Bob Doubles bears a large tick and the date 2014. This is mysterious, as it is the only method so marked. Perhaps I had an abortive scheme to tick each method off as I rang it, but since my first quarter peal of Bob Doubles was in 2012, that seems unlikely.

My partner would roll his eyes at such vagueness. He is scrupulous in his record-keeping and maintains an enormous spreadsheet that lists every tower he has ever rung at, every peal and quarter peal scored, and who it was rung with. This is by no means unusual. There are even some ringers who record every performance lost as well, and the reason – 'conductor error', 'rope broke', 'ringing not good enough'.

Sometimes a performance is unsuccessful for a more colourful reason. Someone's bra strap or waistband may give way, a member of the public might gain access and start chatting to (or haranguing) the ringers, or a worker might appear to service telecommunications equipment mounted on the tower. I even know of one occasion on which the churchwarden called the police because she heard the bells going and thought someone had broken into the tower.

Some of these stories are written up and sent to the ringers' weekly magazine, *The Ringing World*. Though it sounds like the sort of magazine that features as a guest publication on *Have I Got News for You* (as, indeed, it has done), this is actually a much-valued part of the ringing landscape. There are usually several issues knocking around in the ringing room, along with *Diagrams* and the other paraphernalia of tower life. My local tower goes a step further and has stacks of them piled against the walls going back decades, perhaps more. The tower captain keeps looking at them sheepishly and remarking that he 'really ought to get rid of them', but he hasn't yet, and so they stay – a record of a ringing past that chimes with the name-plates above the hooks in the tower wall, each recalling some long-dead gentleman who once hung his hat and coat there before catching hold of his rope. We respect our traditions in the ringing community, for better or worse.

As I write this, of course, all our traditions seem to be under threat. With the United Kingdom in lockdown, and churches closed, the bells have been silent for weeks. This is the longest period without ringing since the end of the Second World War (and the longest period without public worship in England and Wales since the Interdict in the reign of King John). As yet we have no idea when we will be able to ring again, and it seems likely that, when we do go back, there will have to be serious changes in how we go about it. One of the casualties may be the shared tower copy of *Diagrams*, banished as a potential harbourer of the virus. But maybe not. When change ringing began people still lived in fear of the Plague. The

John Bryce, RE, SWE, 'Oranges and Lemons', wood engraving on seven endgrain boxwood blocks

Exercise has weathered much and will, I sincerely hope, survive this too.

So next time you pass a church, just think of that little red or blue book high above your head – not much to look at, hardly even readable, and yet just waiting to have its mysteries made manifest in the joyous pealing of the bells.

MARIANNE FISHER lives and works in rural Monmouthshire. When not on the end of a bell-rope, she is generally to be found gardening, making cider or enjoying the countryside with her pack of whippets.

Church towers are always looking for new ringing recruits, and welcome people of any faith and none. For more information about ringing, and to find your nearest accredited teacher, visit the website of the Central Council of Church Bell Ringers (www.cccbr.org.uk) or the Association of Ringing Teachers (www.ringingteachers.org).

Golden Fire

KATE YOUNG

> The last days of my childhood were also the last days of the village. I belonged to that generation which saw, by chance, the end of a thousand years' life.

I write these words, appropriately enough, in The Woolpack – the Slad pub that once claimed Laurie Lee as its most famous patron – with a pint of cider at my elbow. From one window, the view dips down into a valley, and you can see a path that leads into Stroud, where Lee was born in 1914. From the other, the churchyard, where he is buried beneath the words 'He lies in the valley he loved', is just visible. The cider I am drinking is, inevitably, pressed from local apples: 'golden fire, wine of wild orchids and of that valley and that time and of Rosie's burning cheeks'. It feels, as it often does in The Woolpack, as if the connections with the past, those generations before me who called this place home, are tangible ones, worn into the dark, musty, cider-soaked fabric of the place.

Laurie Lee is inextricably linked to the Five Valleys, this small pocket of the Cotswolds in the West of England. To walk around this area is to walk in his footsteps – there is a Laurie Lee Wood and the Laurie Lee Wild Way, lined with his writings printed on Perspex plaques. There are murals, exhibitions and regular poetry readings and music nights. Fans of Lee's books often visit on a pilgrimage of sorts, to see for themselves the village they already know so well, thanks to *Cider with Rosie* (1959).

Cider with Rosie is the first in a trilogy of memoirs that Laurie Lee wrote between 1959 and 1991. It was followed by *As I Walked Out One*

Midsummer Morning, the tale of his lengthy wanderings on foot and with fiddle, and *A Moment of War*, his writings on the time he spent in Spain during the combative 1930s. All three are worth reading. But, in my university library on the other side of the world, it was his first memoir, a remembering of childhood and the beginnings of adolescence spent in a Cotswold village, with which I fell in love.

Along with his mother, his siblings and older half siblings, Lee moved to a crumbling Slad cottage in 1917, in the shadow of the First World War. A year later, the Armistice brought peace to Europe for the first time in his young life. His father chose not to return to the family after the war, but though his mother spent the rest of her life waiting for him, his absence was barely lamented by his son.

> Meanwhile we lived where he had left us; a relic of his pro-
> vincial youth; a sprawling, cumbersome, countrified brood too
> incongruous to carry with him. He sent us money and we grew
> up without him; and I, for one, scarcely missed him. I was
> perfectly content in this world of women . . .

Lee's recorded memories of those early years are abundant, so rich in detail and so specific that it is impossible not to wonder at the truth of his story; there are parts of the book that read as a sort of self-mythologizing folk tale. Though he was only 3 when the family arrived in Slad, he writes of standing in grass that grew high above his head, of warming fires and celebrations in the village when the war ended.

Though he himself acknowledges that his book is 'a recollection of early boyhood, and some of the facts may be distorted by time', there has been much comment and speculation about the authenticity of his memoirs. He was even sued for libel – the result of some (possibly imagined) memories about a piano factory fire. And it was suggested at one point that *A Moment of War* was entirely fictional, and that Lee had not in fact fought against the fascists in the Spanish Civil War (a claim eventually disproved by his biographer Valerie Grove).

I can't help but feel that these debates seem to miss the point. Regardless of the authenticity of specific details, it is Lee's lyrical and affecting language in *Cider with Rosie* that makes his memoir so memorable; the way he manages to transport us so effectively to Slad, to the icy family home, the fields covered in cowslips, the old schoolroom. His is a book that conjures up a distinct and unmistakable sense of place and time, not just a sequence of events. Regardless of factual accuracy, *Cider with Rosie* has had the impact it has because it feels true to Slad, and to the Cotswolds.

It is easy to think of *Cider with Rosie* as a slice of English nostalgia, a recollection of idyllic rural village life in the early twentieth century.

Quite honestly, this was my memory of the book. But then I spent time rereading it during my recent move from London to Stroud, tracing (in reverse) the journey that Lee himself made on foot as a young man in the 1930s. I was reminded, with a jolt, in amongst the stories of day trips to Weston-super-Mare, and blackberry picking, and carolling in the snow, of the violence, grief and sometimes sheer brutality of village life. Lee writes of the macabre, of murders, attacks, of neighbours destined for the workhouse, with a sort of clear-eyed pragmatism and distinct lack of romanticism.

John Ward

17

Cider with Rosie is undeniably both a lovely book – a beautiful, comforting, inviting picture of the Cotswolds – and an affecting and arresting one, that recalls the work of Thomas Hardy and its pervasive domestic horror, of lives coloured by desperation and despair. We readers find in it great fecundity: trees 'writhed with power, threw off veils of green dust, rose towering into the air, branched into a thousand shaded alleys, became a city for owls and squirrels'. But we're also shown what he calls 'well-prodded horrors' – 'the bird's gaping bones in its cage of old sticks; the black flies in the corner, slimy dead; dry rags of snakes; and the crowded, rotting, silent soaring city of a cat's grub-captured carcass'.

This juxtaposition, the stark contrast between light and dark, has arguably contributed most to the book's longstanding appeal. *Cider with Rosie*, regardless of any literal truth, reads as an emotionally truthful recollection of childhood – of those moments, both hopeful and horrific, tantalizing and terrifying, which shape and form who we grow into. There is an understanding here that it is events both large and seemingly insignificant which provide the threads that will contribute to our comprehension of our world, long before we are ready or able to knit them together.

> Soon the village would break, dissolve, and scatter, become no more than a place for pensioners. It had a few years left, the last of its thousand, and they passed almost without our knowing . . . in motorbike jaunts, in the shadow of the new picture palaces, in trips to Gloucester, once a foreign city, to gaze at the jazzy shops.

For the most part, the village life that Lee writes of has indeed disappeared. The creeping modernity, so present in Lee's post-war narrative, arrived years ago, and now the winding streets of Slad are lined with cars. And yet there is something about the geography of the region that means that Slad will always feel a little as it does in *Cider with Rosie*. During winter, when it snows, we who live in the Five Valleys are left at a bit of a loss. The streets are steep and narrow, too dangerous for vehicles to traverse, and we are forced to venture out on foot for sustenance and supplies. It is in these moments that life here feels most akin to the world about which Lee wrote so vividly.

Even in summer, the valleys provide a uniquely rugged contrast to the otherwise quaint villages of the Cotswolds – it's near impossible to go for a stroll here without finding yourself a little out of breath. Though he was sure that they wouldn't be, Laurie Lee's Slad and Stroud can still be found in small corners and brief moments; in the markets on a Saturday, when orchard owners arrive with cider and crates filled with apples; in the pubs, crammed full with locals listening to music, celebrating and commiserating, making plans and drinking pints; in the hedgerows, still heavy with ripe fruit as summer moves into autumn; at Christmas, when parades wind through the town, and parties and dances are held in the town hall; and in the distinctive curve of each and every street, in this town that I have made my home.

We passed Stroud at last and climbed the valley road, whose every curve our bodies recognized, whose every slant we leaned to, though still half asleep, till we woke to the smell of our houses.

KATE YOUNG is an award-winning writer and cook. She is the author of *The Little Library Cookbook*, *The Little Library Year* and *The Little Library Christmas*, cookbooks which take inspiration from literature.

Laurie Lee's *Cider with Rosie* (272pp), illustrated by John Ward, is now available in a limited and numbered cloth-bound edition of 2,000 copies (subscribers: UK & Eire £17, Overseas £19; non-subscribers: UK & Eire £18.50, Overseas £20.50). All prices include post and packing. Copies may be ordered by post (53 Hoxton Square, London N1 6PB), by phone (020 7033 0258) or via our website www.foxedquarterly.com.

Life Is the Thing

ADAM SISMAN

Recently I decided to reread George Eliot's *Middlemarch* (1871–2). Half a lifetime had passed since my first reading. I remembered how satisfying I had found the book then; now I wondered how I would find it thirty-five years later. Rereading a favourite book can be perilous. Whatever the poet says, one can never quite recapture that 'first fine, careless rapture'. And of course I am not the same person today as I was then.

When I first read *Middlemarch* I was 30, living in a basement flat in King's Cross and pursuing a career in publishing. I thought of myself as mature, though this notion amuses me now. I had been married for five years – indeed, I think it was my late wife who urged me to read it, along with *Anna Karenina, Our Mutual Friend* and a number of other masterpieces that had somehow eluded me during my ill-spent youth. I remember feeling glad I had not discovered the book before, because (so I believed) it would not have meant so much to me at an earlier stage in life. *Middlemarch*, I decided, was a novel about the challenges of adulthood: work and marriage. Though I did not realize it then, the very title of the novel alludes to the middle of life's journey. This is surely what Virginia Woolf meant when she described *Middlemarch* as 'one of the very few English novels written for grown-up people'.

Middlemarch is also the name of a place, the town in the English Midlands (and its surrounding countryside) where the novel is set,

George Eliot, *Middlemarch* (1871–2)
Penguin · Pb · 880pp · £6.99 · ISBN 9780141439549

during the years leading up to the Great Reform Act of 1832. The novel is subtitled 'A Study in Provincial Life', and in its pages Eliot shows us the whole of Middlemarch society, from farmer to squire, maid to mayor, banker to barmaid. This is a society both responding to and (more often) resisting pressure for change – not only from the campaign for political reform, but also from the burgeoning evangelical movement, the inexorable progress of scientific inquiry and the coming of the railways. Sometimes Eliot tells us what Middlemarch thinks, as if the town itself were a character in her story. 'Nobody had anything to say against Mr Tyke, except that they could not bear him, and suspected him of cant.' And as narrator Eliot too is an omnipresent companion, her pithy and often ironic commentary enlivening the narrative throughout. 'When a man has seen the woman whom he would have chosen if he had intended to marry speedily,' she observes at one point, 'his remaining a bachelor will usually depend on her resolution rather than on his.'

Though charged with feeling, *Middlemarch* is almost the antithesis of a romantic novel. George Eliot herself poked fun at what she called 'Silly Novels by Lady Novelists': what she dubbed the 'mind-and-millinery' genre, in which the role of men is largely confined to admiring the 'noble, lovely, and gifted heroine', and in which the affairs of the world, being of little intrinsic interest, take place elsewhere. Such novels usually end happily in a wedding, when the heroine makes a splendid marriage to a handsome, wealthy and (most important) aristocratic man who adores her. By contrast, *Middlemarch* begins with a wedding, followed soon afterwards by another, both of which turn out badly.

At the outset we are introduced to Dorothea Brooke, a serious young woman of independent means, whose plain dress serves only to emphasize her beauty. She and her sister are orphans, in the unreliable care of a bachelor uncle, a man 'of acquiescent temper, miscellaneous opinions, and uncertain vote'. Though intelligent and passionate, Dorothea is unworldly. 'She was usually spoken of as being remarkably clever, but with the addition that her sister Celia had more common-sense.' Dorothea burns with a desire to do something worthwhile: 'something she yearned for by which her life might be filled with action at once rational and ardent'.

Dorothea Brooke is a vividly drawn character – as well she might be, because (as I now appreciate) in her puritanical, priggish zeal she resembles Eliot herself as a young woman; so there is an element of self-mockery in the way in which the novelist portrays her heroine's earnest naïveté. 'The really delightful marriage must be that where your husband was a sort of father, and could teach you even Hebrew, if you wished it.' Dorothea makes a disastrous choice of husband in the dried-up scholar Casaubon, who is indeed old enough to be her father. Everything about him is funereal. 'I feed too much on the inward sources; I live too much with the dead,' he tells her at their first meeting. When he outlines how he envisages their life together, his 'frigid rhetoric' is 'as sincere as the bark of a dog, or the cawing of an amorous rook'. But Dorothea is blind to the warning signs.

Casaubon has long been planning a masterwork, a 'Key to all Mythologies'. For Dorothea, the prospect of becoming his amanuensis in his grand design is alluring. Modern readers may not realize how urgent such a work would have seemed in the intellectual ferment of the mid-Victorian period, when heroic attempts were made to reconcile religion with science, and with discovery more generally. (Those who want to explore this further can read Colin Kidd's fascinating monograph *The World of Mr Casaubon*.) But soon it becomes clear to Dorothea that Casaubon's project is doomed. He does not read German, the language in which Biblical studies and the lost discipline of 'mythography' are most advanced. And Casaubon's thinking has become stale. 'What was fresh to her mind was worn out to his; and such capacity of thought and feeling as had ever been stimulated by the general life of mankind had long shrunk to a kind of dried preparation, a lifeless embalmment of knowledge.'

In parallel with Dorothea's story is that of the idealistic young

Dr Lydgate, who comes to Middlemarch with ambitions to make real advances in medical science and practice. Though not rich, he is well-born, and perhaps overconfident. 'About his ordinary bearing there was a certain fling, a fearless expectation of success, a confidence in his own powers and integrity much fortified by contempt for petty obstacles or seductions of which he had had no experience.'

Middlemarch is suspicious of Lydgate's innovations; and he finds his independence compromised by his association with the dissenting banker Bulstrode, who funds his hospital. At a critical moment, when Lydgate is facing ruin, he is saved by Dorothea's intervention. She is the only person who believes in him. 'What do we live for, if it is not to make life less difficult to each other?' she asks at one point. Riding home afterwards, Lydgate reflects wonderingly on her qualities: 'She seems to have what I never saw in any woman before – a fountain of friendship towards men – a man can make a friend of her.'

By this point Dorothea is a widow. She and Lydgate are well matched: there cannot be many readers of *Middlemarch* who have not wondered whether they are not destined for each other. Earlier Eliot has hinted at the possibility, when she refers to them as 'kindred spirits in the same embroiled medium'. But it is not to be. Like Dorothea, Lydgate has made a bad marriage, to the pretty but shallow Rosamond Vincy, the mayor's daughter, the subject of some of Eliot's most satirical asides. 'She was admitted to be the flower of Mrs Lemon's school, the chief school in the county, where the teaching included all that was demanded in the accomplished female – even to extras, such as the getting in and out of a carriage.'

Lydgate soon finds that she has mastered him. 'There was gathering within him an amazed sense of his powerlessness over Rosamond. His superior knowledge and mental force, instead of being, as he had imagined, a shrine to consult on all occasions, was simply set aside on every practical question.' She is extravagant and wilful. He finds himself trapped, with no time or energy to pursue the studies in which he had once felt such 'a triumphant delight . . . and something like pity for those less lucky men who were not of his profession'. As Caleb Garth, one of the book's most admirable characters, remarks, 'marriage is a taming thing'. Lydgate's dreams fade into bitterness and disappointment.

Perhaps he should have listened more attentively to his friend, the Reverend Farebrother, who reflects on the importance of choosing the right partner. 'A good wife – a good unworldly woman – may really help a man, and keep him more independent.' Farebrother knows just such a woman, Caleb Garth's daughter Mary, and loves her; but she is in love with Fred Vincy, Rosamond's brother, a careless spendthrift, in danger of wasting his prospects. It is Mary's love for Fred that pulls him through, and makes a man of him. After they are married Mary writes a children's book, which everyone in Middlemarch credits to Fred, since he, unlike her, has been to university: 'In this way it was made clear that Middlemarch had never been deceived, and that there was no need to praise anybody for writing a book, since it was always done by somebody else.' Here George Eliot is sharing a little joke with the reader, who will be aware that she is a woman writing books under a male pseudonym.

On my second reading of *Middlemarch* I was more conscious of (or perhaps I had not remembered) a feminist undertone running through the book. 'Women were expected to have weak opinions,' we are told early on, 'but the great safeguard of society and of domestic life was, that opinions were not acted on.' And again: 'a man's mind – what there is of it – has always the advantage of being masculine . . . even his ignorance is of a sounder quality'. Dorothea is said to have 'a great deal of nonsense in her – a flighty sort of Methodistical stuff. But these things wear out of girls.'

Unlike Lydgate, Dorothea finds happiness in a second marriage, to Casaubon's nephew, Will Ladislaw, though it is not the heroic destiny of which she once dreamed. 'Many who knew her, thought it a pity that so substantive and rare a creature should have been absorbed into the life of another, and be only known in a certain circle as a wife and mother.' Yet Eliot's famous conclusion to the book is a form of vindication.

> Her finely touched spirit had still its fine issues, though they were not widely visible. Her full nature, like that river of which Cyrus broke the strength, spent itself in channels which had no great name on the earth. But the effect of her being on those around her was incalculably diffusive: for the growing good of the world is partly dependent on unhistoric acts; and that things are not so ill with you and me as they might have been, is half owing to the number who lived faithfully a hidden life, and rest in unvisited tombs.

I finished reading *Middlemarch* in 2019 feeling much as I had done when I read it in the mid-1980s. It seems to me now, as it seemed to me then, a great novel, one that addresses the practical and fundamental questions that we all have to face.

'People say that life is the thing,' Logan Pearsall Smith once remarked, 'but I prefer reading.' Of course the remark is a quip, meant to make us smile; but perhaps it is worth pausing over. Reading and living are often contrasted; it might plausibly be argued that a life immersed in books is a life not lived. Yet *Middlemarch* is a novel that resolves this apparent antithesis; it is a book that can teach us how to lead richer, fuller lives.

ADAM SISMAN is a writer, specializing in biography. His most recent book is *The Professor and the Parson: A Story of Desire, Deceit and Defrocking* (2019).

A Lost Enchanted World

CHARLOTTE MOORE

Not long ago, in the Tretyakov Gallery in Moscow, I was transfixed by a vast oil painting; Viktor Vasnetsov's *Bogatyrs* (*Men of Power*) – astride their horses, one brown, one black, one white. I felt a thrill of recognition. Here were the three brothers, born to a poor widow in a single night and named Evening, Midnight and Sunrise, 'all three as strong as any of the strong men and mighty bogatyrs who have shaken this land of Russia with their tread'.

The words come from one of the Russian folk tales retold by Arthur Ransome. My mother read *Old Peter's Russian Tales* aloud when I was very young, and they have resonated in my mind ever since. On this, my first, visit to Russia, I realized how much my idea of the country had been shaped and coloured by these stories.

Ransome's most famous contribution to children's literature is, of course, the *Swallows and Amazons* series, but *Old Peter* predates *Swallows and Amazons* by fourteen years. It was his first real success and has never been out of print. Published in 1916, with charmingly appropriate illustrations by Dmitri Mitrokhin, it was the fruit of three years' immersion in Russian folklore. Escaping a turbulent marriage and a stuttering literary career, Ransome arrived in St Petersburg in 1913. 'I had made up my mind to learn Russian to be able to read Russian folklore in the original and to tell those stories in the simple language they seemed to need,' wrote Ransome, and indeed the strength of the *Tales* lies in their simplicity.

Arthur Ransome, *Old Peter's Russian Tales* (1916)
Blurb · Hb · 198pp · £16 · ISBN 9781389442179

Old Peter is a peasant who lives in a hut in the forest with his two orphan grandchildren, Vanya and Maroosia, his 'little pigeons'. This is the framing device; Peter tells the stories to the children, and their comments and reactions, and the glimpses Ransome gives us of their way of life, embed the fantasy in satisfyingly solid reality. Talking fish, a cloud castle built of red roses, a mountain made of salt, magic tablecloths, giant witch-babies with iron teeth, become tangible components of a rich and strange culture, all the more vivid thanks to historical hindsight; a year after publication, revolution decreed that the certainties of Old Peter's Russia, ruled by an all-seeing 'little father Tzar', must be obliterated.

In childhood I wasn't aware of the historic value of Ransome's collection, one of the last outsider narratives of pre-Revolution peasant life. But I was acutely aware of the scalp-prickling contrast between the snug hut made of pine logs ('You could see the marks of the axe') and warmed by the stove on which the children slept 'warm as little baking cakes' with, outside, the endless wolf-haunted forest, the silence of deep snow broken by the crashing sounds 'as the tired branches flung down their loads of snow'. In comes Old Peter, stamping the snow off his boots. He hangs up his gun, holds the children close inside his sheepskin coat until they squeal; he makes tea in the samovar, they eat soup with their wooden spoons. Old Peter lights his pipe (Ransome was himself a heroic pipe-smoker); it's full of 'very strong tobacco, called Mahorka, which has a smell like hot tin'. The evening ritual leads to the magic moment when the storytelling begins, the stories filling the hut like the curls of pipe-smoke and the steam from the samovar.

Faith Jaques

The titles tell you how marvellous the tales will be. 'The Silver Saucer and the Transparent Apple'; 'The Fool of the World and the Flying Ship'; 'Prince Ivan, the Witch Baby, and the

Little Sister of the Sun'; 'The Fire-Bird, the Horse of Power, and the Princess Vasilissa' – all irresistible to an imaginative child. The narratives follow the patterns of folk tales the world over. Stepmothers are wicked, youngest sons prove braver and more resourceful than their greedy older brothers, people and events come in threes, you can (usually) trust a talking animal. There's a universal folk-morality; doing a good turn will save you in the end, black deeds come to light through beneficent Nature, pride comes before a fall. '"This", said Old Peter, "is a story about wanting more than enough."' And everywhere there are enchanted realms and beings – both bad and good – in the air, under the water, deep in the earth, in the heart of the forest, just out of reach. But only just.

Fairy stories have happy endings. Of course they do. They raise fears and problems, and resolve them – that's what they're for. Arthur Ransome's versions are no exception. But he's quite tough, and he doesn't smooth away everything that's uncomfortable. 'Little Master Misery' is about alcoholism, that dark danger at the heart of Russian peasant life. Baba Yaga, the cannibal witch, is outwitted by the 'little girl with the kind heart', but not killed; she returns to her hut on hen's legs, 'gnashing her teeth and screaming with rage and disappointment', but we know she'll re-emerge some day. The sad childless couple who made themselves a snow girl cannot keep her –

> Good-bye, ancient ones, good-bye,
> Back I go across the sky;
> To my motherkin I go –
> Little daughter of the snow

sings the snow girl as she disappears, leaving behind her only a pool of water in front of the stove, 'and a fur hat, and a little coat, and little red boots were lying in it'. This is too much for Vanya and Maroosia. Old Peter has to console them with a hint that the snow girl might one day return. Even as an adult, I find I can't type these words without emotion.

Writing fairy tales is the only (literary) subject 'that it is possible to excel in without a degree', the non-graduate Ransome told his mother. He learned his Russian from children's primers, and from travelling by train, sledge and on foot, listening to how ordinary people talked. The *Tales* have an incantatory rhythm; for almost two years Ransome repeated them to himself as he walked, before he wrote them down. Open the book at any page and the rhythm swells to the surface: 'The sea piled itself into waves with crests of foam, and the fire-bird came flying from the other side of the world'; 'Wake me, dear father, from a bitter dream, by fetching water from the well of the Tzar'; 'Eaten the father, eaten the mother, and now to eat the little brother'. There's colour, too – pure strong red and green and blue, and the feel of fur and frost and wood and metal. And, as with any good book for children, there's fascinating food, black bread and kasha and red kisel jelly. Ransome makes sure that all the senses of his young readers are involved.

Brilliantly, he ends the collection not with magic but with a real event, the christening of Vanya and Maroosia's baby cousin. This gives Ransome an opportunity to describe Old Peter's cart with its larch-pole springs, the gun which is his present for baby Nikolai ('he shall be a forester, and a good shot, and you cannot begin too early'), the carved timbers of the village huts, the church with its bright green cupolas and icons. The baby 'goes right into the water, not once, but three times', and is anointed with sacred ointment; the priest 'cut a little pinch of fluff from the baby's head, and rolled it into a pellet with the ointment, and threw the pellet in the holy water. And after that baby was carried solemnly three times round the holy water. The priest blessed it and prayed for it; and there it was, a true little Russian.' Magic and religion are shown to be intimately intertwined.

Baby Nikolai 'knew all the world belonged to him because he was so very young'. How could he, or his real-life counterpart, or indeed Ransome, his creator, have foreseen how much that world would change? The gulf between his infancy and his Stalinist future was unimaginable and unbridgeable. But though Ransome describes peasant customs with affection and respect, he was no apologist for the Romanov regime that was so soon to collapse. On the contrary, he knew Lenin well, was in love with Trotsky's secretary (she became his second wife) and was the principal British eyewitness of the events of 1917. Was he a double agent? Probably yes, up to a point. Bruce Lockhart, the British diplomat and secret agent whose attempt to stymie the revolution failed partly because some of his co-conspirators were in the pay of the Bolsheviks, wrote that 'Ransome was a Don Quixote with a walrus moustache, a sentimentalist who could always be relied on to champion the underdog, and a visionary whose imagination had been fired by the revolution. He was on excellent terms with the Bolsheviks and frequently brought us information of the greatest value.'

When Ransome tramped through the forests gathering material for *Old Peter*, perhaps he had a sense that, as the Horse of Power tells his rider the brave young archer, 'the trouble is not yet; the trouble is to come'. Eventually he would hole up in the Lake District and entertain a generation with boats and campfires and treasure maps. Thank goodness *Old Peter's Russian Tales* survives, a shining doorway into a lost world.

CHARLOTTE MOORE is an author of fiction and non-fiction. She lives in East Sussex and runs workshops on life writing and poetry reading. Her poetry anthology, *The Magic Hour*, has just been published by Short Books.

Strangely Prophetic

ANTHONY LONGDEN

I always take particular pleasure in people's stories about how they discover books.

For me, the process is quite conventional, more often than not the result of a trip to the London Library, through word of mouth, via *Slightly Foxed*, or a profitable hour or two spent in a favourite second-hand bookshop. There is one exception in my experience, though: a discovery made thanks to a devastating fire at a country house.

Around 3.30 p.m. on 30 August 1989, alarms sounded at Uppark, the imposing National Trust property perched high up on the South Downs in West Sussex.

The house, dating back to 1690, was being extensively repaired. Workers welding lead on the roof failed to notice that wooden beams underneath had caught fire. The result was devastating – the blaze ripped through the ancient fabric, destroying the upper floors and everything in them.

Thanks to the quick thinking of shocked National Trust staff and firefighters, a great deal of furniture and other items were saved from the flames. Then debate raged as to whether or not Uppark should be restored to its former glory. In the end the Trust went ahead with the restoration, and the house was reopened to the public in 1995.

Those horrendous images on the television news stayed with me, and, having known the house as it was before the fire, I was deter-

---

Simon Harcourt-Smith, *The Last of Uptake, or The Estranged Sisters* (1942), is out of print but we can obtain second-hand copies.

mined to see its restoration for myself. On that visit (and I have to say the Trust has done a wonderful job), I bought a copy of *Uppark Restored* by Christopher Rowell and John Martin Robinson. It carries a foreword by the then Director-General of the National Trust, Martin Drury, which recalls another, fictional house destroyed by fire:

> 'Next there came a low rumble, sparks flying like fireworks . . . and the whole of Uptake was roaring and crackling.' These words described the climax of a story published in 1942, strangely pre-figuring the fire that ravaged Uppark forty-five years later. *The Last of Uptake* by Simon Harcourt-Smith, with illustrations by Rex Whistler, is a picturesque novel about a country house called Uptake, the home of two old ladies, the last of their line, who set it on fire to prevent it from passing into other hands. Rex Whistler's tailpiece shows the sisters driving away in their carriages with the great house ablaze in the distance.

Uppark, too, was home to two old ladies at the end of the nineteenth century, the owner Miss Fetherstonhaugh and her companion. Miss Fetherstonhaugh bequeathed it to the son of a neighbour, Admiral the Honourable Sir Herbert Meade-Fetherstonhaugh, who inherited it in 1931. He spent the next thirty-five years preserving the house, which later passed to the National Trust.

But what of this book, *The Last of Uptake*, and its Rex Whistler connection?

Published by Batsford, it's a neat, square volume, on that wartime paper that so often yellows appealingly with age and feels almost like felt. The obvious draw is its wonderful illustrations. I always think of Whistler alongside those other distinctive mid-twentieth century giants, Ravilious, Bawden, Laider – better known as the cartoonist, 'Pont' – and Ardizzone.

Whistler's work here is simply lovely, bringing house, grounds and characters vividly to life. It does not, however, eclipse Harcourt-

Smith's finely crafted tale of internecine sibling rivalry and creeping decay. Apart from the grim sisters, Lady Tryphena and Lady Deborah, we meet Plummett the housekeeper, Hake the butler, and Titmarsh the gardener. All, of course, are completely devoted to the crumbling sisters and their equally crumbling home.

You can almost imagine Hake the butler being covered with a thick layer of dust:

Rex Whistler

> He had come to look very ancient and frail these last years; and he was growing, what one could only call, a little soft in the head; but the other day, hadn't they caught him, with a gigantic rusty pair of snuffers, trying to snuff the gas lamps in the Chinese saloon?

Harcourt-Smith, though quite prolific in his own way, is something of a literary enigma. His voice can be briefly heard thanks to a letter he sent to the *TLS* in 1953, in defence of his book on the Borgias, *The Marriage at Ferrara*, in which he hits back forcibly at allegations of plagiarism from a rival historian, but *The Last of Uptake* is entirely different from the rest of his output, which was scholarly and factual.

I want you to read this delightful little book, so no spoilers here, but his scene-setting of Uptake is a delight:

> the mist became tangled in the elms, twined under the pediment, set the stucco sweating. Drops of moisture as big as grapes fell and burst on the flags in the colonnade; at times there fell with them bits of swallows' nests, or the plaster tip of some Emperor's nose. It all made a terrible mess . . .

The grounds are dilapidated, filled with mouldering ornaments, and even some extraordinary automata in various states of collapse, constant reminders of a happy past the sisters can never retrieve.

There is a uniquely compelling atmosphere of decline permeating the book. Apart from the fact that it appeared in the dark days of a war (a war that claimed the life of Whistler), the fall of the country house and the 'servant crisis' were already well under way by the time it came out. Stately homes were being lost thanks to a combination of genteel poverty, crippling death duties and the dearth of domestic staff; four centuries of architectural heritage were swept away in the space of four decades or so.

In publishing terms, *The Last of Uptake* was also a casualty of war. Rebecca West knew it well and lamented its limited success: 'The book has long been a treasure of mine, and I have always thought it a great misfortune that it failed to be recognized as a classic because it was published during the war.'

Slim it may be, but this is a neglected volume that will haunt you long after you have put it down.

Journalist and crisis communications specialist ANTHONY LONGDEN gamely continues to fight a losing battle against the steadily rising tide of books that threatens to engulf his home.

Rex Whistler

The Thrillers You Keep

FRANCES DONNELLY

Ink has been spilt debating when genre novels become literary fiction. My rule of thumb for recognizing the best in any genre is this: notice what books you keep, won't lend and need to reread every few years. In detective fiction, for me, this means the books of Ross Macdonald, whose PI hero, Lew Archer, investigated murder and excess in post-war California.

Ross Macdonald was the pen name of the Scottish Canadian-born writer Kenneth Millar. He wrote *The Moving Target* because he needed money. It was 1949, he was 32 and already he knew his commercial future lay in writing crime novels. But his two first attempts, followed by the ill-advised 'serious novel', had generated little income. He wanted to pull his weight financially – his wife, Margaret Millar, was already a successful crime writer. He needed a quick, colourful, saleable book.

Post-war America had an unquenchable appetite for stories about strong capable men working as private eyes. Macdonald's central character, Lew Archer, a divorced ex-policeman and private investigator 'working for 65 dollars a day', was a fictional hero for the time. Macdonald's publishers were grudging with an advance but the critics did not stint their praise. 'You can put this on your Chandler, Hammett shelf and it won't look out of place' was the critical consensus. Furthermore, Millar had enjoyed writing it. From the outset he acknowledged how much of himself was in the character of Lew

---

Ross Macdonald's *The Moving Target* (1949) and Tom Nolan's 1999 biography are both out of print, but we can try to obtain second-hand copies

Archer. 'I'm not Archer,' he later famously remarked, 'but Archer is me.'

The Moving Target is written with more than a passing nod to Raymond Chandler's *The Big Sleep* (1939). Both open with a PI summoned to a mansion to find a missing person. But Chandler's client, General Sternwood, wants someone found whom he likes and misses. Lew Archer, on the other hand, has to find Ralph Sampson, an absent millionaire, unlovingly described by his wife as 'Half-man, half-alligator, half-bear trap, with a piggy bank where his heart should be. But I'm twenty years younger and I'm going to survive him.'

The best thrillers share two factors. First, a strongly defined main character who stands for morality in a corrupted world. Lew recognizes that he's only one step away from the bad guys but he still wants justice. Also, he's an outsider. He likes entering other people's lives rather than having commitments of his own. Hence the divorced status. Second, he has to work against a landscape that intrigues us and moves the plot forward. California – 'a sunny place for shady people' as another writer memorably put it – takes Archer through post-war LA excess in his search for Ralph: sharp glimpses of film sound stages, louche piano bars and questionable cults. The dialogue is crisp, there's plenty of action, guns are carried and used, and Lew reveals himself as good at his job. So far, so in tune with Chandler and Hammett. But what was to differentiate him from them was that Archer had a social conscience. Ralph Sampson, already oil-rich, turns out to be funding a people-smuggling racket exploiting Mexican immigrants. Archer comments: 'It makes it easier to gouge people if you don't admit they're human.'

Hammett wrote five books, Chandler wrote seven, but Millar as Ross Macdonald wrote eighteen Lew Archer novels. They paid well but there was something more to this proliferation than sheer facility. He was drawn to crime writing because he recognized evil in himself. Tom Nolan's fine biography *Ross Macdonald* (1999) describes a fractured childhood that created two personalities – a quiet, bookish, brilliant student, and a dirt-poor, unsupervised, furious boy who had sex from the age of 8, was getting drunk at 12 and habitually fought and stole.

It took a conscious act of will in his late teenage years to reject his dark side and put himself in the box of sanity – and stay there. He married early and stayed married. He applied his ferocious intelligence to writing successful detective fiction, determined to be a better parent than his own father had been. Jack Millar, son of a Scottish immigrant to Canada, had edited newspapers in the Old West, lived with Indians in the Northwest Territories, and befriended Japanese fishing families in Vancouver. But through bad luck, bad health and bad judgement he ended up in the poorhouse, leaving his wife and son destitute.

A start like this will leave a mark on any child. Certain themes occur again and again in Millar's intricate and finely crafted plots. The anguished longing for a lost father. The resulting man-boys who can't achieve maturity because they lack the example to lead them there. Faultlines caused by family secrets that will inevitably fracture under pressure. Young people who, lacking any sense of meaning in life, are seduced by the hope of 'something utterly new. Something bright and shiny in the road. A moving target.'

What draws me back to his books? Fizzing dialogue. Poetic evocation of the California landscape. Witty, wonderfully perceptive observation of character. But it's so much more than just brilliant writing. Troubled, failing people are never dismissed with a wisecrack. Their humanity is noted and honoured. Pick up any Ross Macdonald thriller and you'll find it's underpinned by a deep compassion.

FRANCES DONNELLY still lives in Suffolk and still bakes. She was about to move this January and is profoundly grateful that she didn't. When lockdown ceases she plans to adopt a retired Irish greyhound.

Put That in Your Pipe . . .

LAURENCE SCOTT

One wouldn't normally associate a book on pipes and pipe-smoking with deceit, guilt and posterior discomfort. This is how it happened.

It was 1964. I was a scholastically challenged 14-year-old from north London who had just undergone double maths. Still dazed, I'd wandered off to the back of the bike sheds where I came across Howard Payne and his cronies furtively dispatching a packet of Gauloises.

Payne was a schoolboy thug with whom I had nothing in common except that it was he who occupied my position at the bottom of the class on those rare occasions when I vacated it. His favourite trick was to feign largesse by offering a cigarette to the unwary. If you refused, or failed to smoke it without coughing, you would be ridiculed and your shins remodelled.

As I'd never smoked anything before and was rather attached to Nature's provision in the lower-leg department, I decided to put him off with the following: 'No thank you, Payne,' I said. 'I used to smoke cigarettes when I was young but I now prefer the more mature smoke afforded by a good pipe.' There followed a torrent of abuse and the fixing of a date after the Easter holidays when I would be required to back up my boast or suffer the aforementioned.

The following morning I was in my local library enquiring about the Government Assisted Passage Scheme to Australia when I happened upon a book written by a tobacconist called Dunhill, a name

---

Alfred Dunhill, *The Pipe Book* (1924), is out of print but we can try to obtain second-hand copies.

I'd seen on some of my father's pipes. *The Pipe Book* sets out to trace the global history of pipes and pipe-smoking from the sixteenth century to the early decades of the twentieth. Full of easily parrotable facts and insights, comprehensive descriptions of the pipes themselves, photographs and line drawings, it seemed the ideal tool with which to fake expertise and get the better of Payne. I took it home and started reading.

In the 1920s, tobacco consumption in the UK reached its peak and so did Alfred Dunhill's sales, but he was no ordinary tobacconist. Born in Hornsey, north London, in 1872 and privately educated, at the age of 32 he invented the ingenious 'windshield pipe' to assist smokers on bicycles and in open-topped cars. By the time *The Pipe Book* was published in 1924 he had become a highly regarded collector of pipes, a successful retailer of bespoke tobacco blends and products, and a manufacturer of high-quality pipes bearing his name. He had shops in London, Paris and New York, a royal warrant from Edward, Prince of Wales, and a customer list that included Siegfried Sassoon, Winston Churchill and the actor Basil Rathbone who, incidentally, smoked a Dunhill briar during his first on-screen outing as Sherlock Holmes.

An elementary investigation revealed that I had insufficient pocket-money to purchase *any* pipe, let alone a Dunhill; and as my father's briars were displayed in constant view on a wooden table-top rotunda next to his armchair, a covert operation to borrow one of his was out of the question. As indeed was purchasing tobacco: since 1908 it had been illegal for anyone under the age of 16 to buy or consume tobacco products.

My eye, however, fell on the chapter entitled 'Makeshift Pipes and Tobacco', in which Dunhill explains that it was once common for people to assemble an ad-hoc pipe whenever they fancied a smoke. For example, about five hundred years ago the Montbutto tribe from the Congo used the midrib of a plantain leaf 'bored all through with a stick' into which they inserted 'a plantain leaf twisted up into a cornet'. In the absence of tobacco the cornet was filled with dried local flora and ignited. I discovered, too late, that this method had sickening consequences when applied to my parents' shrubbery and herbaceous border.

I asked my father why smoking a pipe didn't make him feel bilious. He replied that smoke from pipe-tobacco is rarely inhaled into the lungs, but drawn into the mouth where the mucus membranes absorb the chemicals in the smoke and produce the desired effect. As I had no pipe-tobacco to inhale or draw in, a fresh approach was needed, and I put in place a simple three-part plan:

1. Retrieve from tool-shed one of Father's empty tobacco tins.
2. At night while parents sleep move small quantity of tobacco from Father's tobacco-pouch to said tin.
3. Return to bed with said tin, leaving Father none the wiser.

The sequel was unexpected. I spent a sleepless night racked with guilt while conducting an internal debate on whether 'Theft Is Always Wrong'. Then, a few minutes before dawn, I arrived at the following conclusion: 'If thief intends to replace stolen tobacco as soon as he can save sufficient pocket money and is old enough to do so, then it isn't stealing but borrowing.' Ditto Swan Vestas from my father's desk drawer.

Dunhill's chapter 'Indian Pipes and Pipe Mysteries' contained the intriguing information that some native Americans would fashion a smoking device from the earth itself. Various methods were used including 'building a bowl on the ground from a clod of wet clay, and thrusting into the side of it a long hollow reed to serve as a stem'. When in possession of an actual pipe they regarded it with reverence. 'It was seen as the instrument by which the breath of man ascended to God through fragrant smoke, carrying with it the prayer or aspiration of the smoker.' Hence the common use of a pipe to cast spells on an enemy, the smoke wafted in the direction of the Hated One. (This raised a pleasing prospect of Payne's body parts dropping off.)

The Omaha were one of many tribes who used pipes and pipe-smoking to help them in the making of decisions, such as whether the tribe should go to war or maintain the peace. Dunhill has a line-drawing which shows the war-pipe – a surprisingly plain and simple affair with a straight stem about two feet long made of hollowed-out ash-wood, and a simple bowl adorned with just a small totemic shape where it meets the stem. The peace-pipe, however, while similar in size and construction to the war-pipe, was elaborately and colourfully decorated with bird feathers and animal hair, each tuft of hair and barb of feather so steeped in totemic significance that a stranger needed only a quick glance to identify the pipe-owner's tribe.

The other twelve chapters of the book – unread by me in 1964 but read with fascination fifty years later – are either organized by locale, such as 'Pipes of the Far North' (bowls carved from stone and walrus bone by the Eskimo, or Inuit), or by type, such as 'Water Pipes' (cooling and cleansing the smoke by passing it through water, popular in Africa and Egypt). The book's final chapter, 'The Modern Briar', brings us to the early decades of the twentieth century and the answer to the question: Why is it that so many pipe-smokers choose a pipe made from briar wood?

The root of the *bruyère* bush, indigenous to the whole margin of the western Mediterranean, was discovered during the seventeenth century to be a durable hardwood capable of resisting heat and therefore cool to the hand. That same durability makes it suitable for machining into the standardized shapes used for mass production; and the briar's tight grain becomes very attractive when buffed and polished.

When Dunhill was researching his book, 30 million briar-pipes were manufactured in France every year, 25 million of which were exported to Britain. 'The twentieth-century connoisseur', writes

Dunhill, 'selects his pipe for the excellence of its workmanship, the correctness of its proportions and, above all, for the delicate beauty of its flawless, straight-grained bowl.' Ideal for display on a wooden table-top rotunda.

On the first morning of the new school term, I put my tobacco and Swan Vestas into my satchel, ensured my socks were securely gartered, and cycled off to school ready for Payne. A small crowd had gathered, Payne and his cronies at the front smoking something possibly Turkish, and about a dozen first-years behind. I headed straight for the groundsman's hut and emerged carrying a garden trowel. 'I shall now demonstrate earth-smoking,' I announced. 'It is an ancient technique described by Alfred Dunhill in his authoritative work *The Pipe Book* and practised by the legendary Red Indians – Crazy Horse, Tonto and Sitting Bull.'

I dropped to my knees and, with the help of the trowel, assembled from the soil a six-inch volcano. Into its top I tipped the tobacco

from my tin and, into its side, fashioned an aperture through which tobacco smoke could be drawn. I struck a Swan Vesta and put a flame to the tobacco. I then lay belly down, cupped my hands about the aperture, put my mouth to my hands and, without a single cough, drew in.

My first exhalation brought forth an *Ooh!* from the first-years; the second an *Aaah!*; at the third they gave a round of enthusiastic applause. Payne, his contorted lips struggling with a half-formed monosyllable, reluctantly stepped forward and patted me on the shoulder.

Unfortunately, I had failed to notice a sudden thinning of the crowd and the equally sudden arrival of P. W. Travers (Headmaster) and F. Nobbs (Groundsman). After waiting patiently for my explanations to cease, Travers remarked that he too had read *The Pipe Book* and was the proud owner of a seventeenth-century Red Indian 'pipe of peace'.

'May I suggest', I said, 'that you light up immediately and draw in several times before considering any future action.'

*

To this day pipe-collectors the world over consider *The Pipe Book* essential reading. As tobacco sales in Britain waned, the Dunhill company built on its reputation for well-made products, and successfully diversified into the luxury goods market. Alfred Dunhill FRSA died in Worthing, Sussex, in 1959; he was survived by his wife, two sons and the global brand which bears his name.

LAURENCE SCOTT lives in a small town in south-west Scotland. His poetry pops up occasionally in magazines and journals, his prose in *Slightly Foxed*.

A Merry Malady

RICHARD PLATT

Let's begin with a brief quiz. Have you ever arrived home, triumphant with glee over your latest bookshop find, only to discover that you already have the book you just purchased? Have you ever attempted to bring home unobserved a stack of newly purchased books, and thus avoid the censorious lift of the eyebrows of loved ones which so often greets your latest acquisitions? Have you ever begun reading a book you've been looking forward to for years, even decades, only to discover your own notes in the margins? (If so, you are a bibliolathas.) Are you on first-name terms with the staff of three bookshops or more? Have you ever had to reinforce a sagging floor because of the weight of your books? Have you ever had to add a room on to your home or move to a larger one to accommodate them?

If you can answer yes to at least three of these questions you will understand why book collecting is the only hobby to have a disease named after it: bibliomania. You will also appreciate the allure of a title like *The Anatomy of Bibliomania*.

My discovery of this treatise by Holbrook Jackson was not serendipitous, for in a bookshop, as every bibliophile knows, there are no accidents. There is only Destiny. It sat on the dusty shelf at eye-level: a siren song in two glorious volumes, bound in red buckram, the 1931 Soncino Press first edition, number 537 from a limited edition of 1,000 copies (alas, not one of the 48 copies on hand-made paper), 8vo, gilt top edges, minor fading to spines, no foxing, tanning or

Holbrook Jackson, *The Anatomy of Bibliomania* (1931)
Franklin Classics · Hb · 674pp · £26.95 · ISBN 9780343160715

bumping to extremities, text block clean and tight, hinges strong, no previous owner's inscription or bookplate.

Modelled on Robert Burton's *The Anatomy of Melancholy*, both in format and in its deliciously pedantic early-seventeenth-century turn of phrase, it is an exhaustive pastiche of everything ever written that's worth saying (as well as a few things that might have been better left unsaid) about the nature and allure of books and the characteristics, not always flattering, of the people who treasure them. Jackson wrote dozens of books, many on bookish subjects (see *SF* no. 16), but this surely is his magnum opus.

A sampling of the Table of Contents will illustrate why the whole reads like the bibliophilic equivalent of Aladdin's cave: *Of Letter Ferrets and Book Sots*; *A Cure for Pedantry*; *Of the Bibliophagi or Book-eaters* (these are, mostly, metaphors, though the legendary bookdealer A. S. W. Rosenbach attributed the scarcity of first editions of *Alice's Adventures in Wonderland* to their having been eaten by children); *Liberating the Soul of Man*; *Reading at the Toilet* (a fine bit of bathos, this); *The Book-borrower* and *All Manner of Biblioklepts* (a pervasive and insuperable strain on countless friendships); *Defence of Fine Bindings* (as if one were needed); *Book Ghouls*(!); and *On Parting with Books* (material to make even a stout heart quail).

Having whetted our appetite, we turn the page to discover 'The Author to the Reader', one of those lengthy, discursive and often unnecessary prefaces one is inclined to skip, but then we read this:

Gentle Reader, I presume thou wilt be very inquisitive to know what antic or personate actor it is that so insolently intrudes upon this common theatre to the world's view, arrogating, as you will soon find, another man's style and method: whence he is, why he does it, and what he has to say. 'Tis a proper attitude, and the questions clear and reasonable in themselves, but I owe thee no answer, for if the contents please thee 'tis well; if they be useful, 'tis an added value; if neither, pass on . . .

Pass on? 'Arrogate, Sir!' say I. This is an antic and personate actor I can cosy up to, and for the next 600 pages the tone never falters; nor does Jackson's formidable vocabulary. How often do we confront words like *operose, fardel, erewhile, dizzards, solatium, welter, collectanca, peradventure, belike* and (my favourite) the musical *gallimaufry*? Yet all these are to be found just in the preface.

Jackson's ardent pedantry lends itself as happily to the joy of books as it does to his take-no-prisoners attacks on the creatures who misuse them or, worse still, those who pretend to a familiarity with a book they have not read, for whom he reserves a special venom. These are the book pscittacists (now *there's* a word for you), the people who repeat, parrot-like, what they have heard others say of books or what they have gleaned from dust-wrapper blurbs and reviews. The range and depth of Jackson's own reading and his facility for unearthing the most apropos quotations are astonishing. He begins his rant, 'Vain and Pedantic Reading Condemned', by marshalling Crabbe, Montaigne and Samuel Butler.

> There are others . . . that eschew all reading except for vainglory, *Who read huge works to boast what ye have read*, to disport their second-hand stock of ideas and information, *for a fading greedy glory, to cousin and delude the foolish world*; to peacock themselves at large, like Aesop's daw in borrowed feathers. Among them are others who *Affect all books of past and modern ages,/ But read no further than the title-pages*.

One thinks of *Finnegans Wake* or the novels of Thomas Pynchon. I know there are people who have actually made it through *Finnegans Wake*, and even liked it, but for everyone who has said so honestly there are hundreds who have told a whopping fib. As for Pynchon, I myself trudged to the end of *Mason and Dixon* because a friend gave me a copy, raved about it, and truly had read it himself and loved it. It was a journey more arduous than that of the intrepid surveyors through storm, swamp and wilderness. Never again. Life is short, and

'Holy Cow! What kind of crazy people used to live here anyway?'

there are limits to friendship. Still, as Pope wrote, I concede that judgements are like watches. None go just alike yet each believes his own.

Chock-a-block with quotations, aphorisms and anecdotes, all lovingly and meticulously footnoted, *The Anatomy of Bibliomania* is a treasure-trove of whimsy, revelry, vituperative eloquence and the disconcertingly weird. There is Edward Gibbon, who swapped a copy of his *Decline and Fall* for a hogshead of Madeira. There is the man who wanted to perform a Christian marriage for an aboriginal couple in Central America, but as they knew no English and he had no bible, he officiated at their nuptials by reading aloud a chapter from *Tristram Shandy*. There is the story of a Dr O'Rell, who claimed to have discovered the cause of the book-lover's disease in a *bacillus librorum*, which when injected into the femoral artery of a cat caused it to eat a copy of Rabelais. Then there are the aforementioned book ghouls, the people who destroy books to turn them into storage boxes for cigars, chocolates and notepaper.

They are no better than body-snatchers, desecrators of the temple, vain, tawdry, callous, whether sellers of such monuments of destruction or buyers of them, biblioclasts and dolts to boot, necrofils of a sort; beside them the *naïfs* who use dummy books are princes of intelligence, nay bibliophiles of the blood, though dizzards . . .

Happily, Jackson did not live to see *Reader's Digest* Condensed Books. They would no doubt have reminded him of Robert Burton, who wrote in a far coarser context that starving dogs will eat dirty puddings.

Many years ago, before my own bibliophilic illness began seriously to take hold, I kept my books in a small room about six feet wide and perhaps twelve feet long, the two longer walls lined with bookshelves, leaving room for a floor lamp and a comfortable chair in the centre. Soon I began double shelving, removed the chair and placed a double-width bookcase down the centre of the room. This left two passageways that were each perhaps nine inches wide.

Thus, if I wanted a book I had to move into the room sideways, like a crab, and if I discovered the book I wanted was behind me, I had to back out and turn around. Books near the floor were more problematic. There was no room to crouch, so I had to lie down and slink in, caterpillar-style. When a friend from London, herself a book dealer, saw my little room, there was, as the novelists say, a pregnant pause. After a deep breath, her eyes grew wider and her face contorted into something between a smile and a grimace. 'Oh, you've got it *bad*,' she said.

And so, Gentle Reader, if you have yourself experienced one of those moments – and if you're reading this you almost certainly have – you will find *The Anatomy of Bibliomania* the most congenial and empathetic of bedside companions.

As he lives a rich fantasy life, RICHARD PLATT is attempting to pare down his library and resist the temptation of new acquisitions, the exception, of course, being Slightly Foxed Editions.

Something Wicked This Way Comes

SAM LEITH

My dad turned me on to Ray Bradbury. The short stories had captivated him in his late teens and early twenties, and on his shelf was a two-volume Grafton paperback collection of them.

There was a waft in them of something dark and strange and menacing and mysterious and infinitely delicious. Picture me, a knock-kneed ten-year-old bookworm in the anaesthetized suburban Surrey of the mid-1980s, taking down from the shelf the first of those two volumes. Its cover had THE STORIES OF RAY BRADBURY in large black block capitals on a red background and, underneath, even larger and in yellow capitals, VOLUME I. Or rather: VOLUME, and then, underneath and fully half the height of the cover, the numeral I pointed upwards like a rocket-ship.

And what a rocket-ship it was. It took me to dozens and dozens of other worlds. Bradbury is a poet of the *unheimlich*, or unhomely. He transports and unsettles. On the one hand, he has an almost miraculous fecundity of imagination – he's thought to have written as many as 400 short stories, though nobody seems to be able to put a precise figure on it. On the other, he returns again and again to the same set of vibes, the same themes – the sinister carnival blowing into town, disrupting the safety of the Mid-western America of his small-town childhood in Waukegan, Illinois; the vampiric visitor; the dinosaur; the monster; the lonely beauty of Mars.

The introduction to those volumes was called 'Drunk – and in

A collection of the short stories of Ray Bradbury (1912–2012) is available in two paperback volumes from HarperVoyager, at £20 each.

Charge of a Bicycle', and it is at once memoir and manifesto. The way he expresses his relation to his stories is that the muse chased him, rather than vice versa: 'My stories have led me through my life. They shout, I follow. They run up and bite me on the leg – I respond by writing down everything that goes on during the bite. When I finish, the idea lets go, and runs off.'

Bradbury describes a writing life in which he followed his childhood obsessions through a lifelong trip which he identifies as 'exactly one half terror, exactly one half exhilaration', which is a good description of how the stories strike a reader. Looked at from some angles, he's a science-fiction writer; from others the writer of horror stories without whom Stephen King could never have got started.

> When I was three my mother snuck me in and out of movies two or three times a week. My first film was Lon Chaney in *The Hunchback of Notre Dame*. I suffered permanent curvature of the spine and of my imagination that day a long time ago in 1923. From that hour on, I knew a kindred and wonderfully grotesque compatriot of the dark when I saw one. I ran off to see all the Chaney films again and again to be deliciously frightened. The Phantom of the Opera stood astride my life with his scarlet cape. And when it wasn't the Phantom it was the terrible hand that gestured from behind the bookcase in *The Cat and the Canary*, bidding me to come find more darkness hid in books.

Bradbury is a sci-fi writer with the soul of a poet and the nous of a travelling salesman. Just look at the titles. They were frequently ripped off from poets – but what poets, and how stylishly ripped off! 'Dark They Were, And Golden Eyed'; 'The Golden Apples of the Sun'; 'Dandelion Wine'; 'The Illustrated Man'; 'There Will Come Soft Rains'; 'The Wonderful Ice Cream Suit'; 'Something Wicked This Way Comes'.

When I say he has the nous of a travelling salesman, I mean, too, that he approached his work as a jobbing writer in the age of the pulps

– just a fantastically talented one. He spliced old short stories together and turned them into novels (as did Raymond Chandler), reworked them, repackaged them, resold them. *The Illustrated Man* and *The Martian Chronicles* are both 'fix-ups': short stories patched together and threaded into a novel. The novel in linked short stories that has had such a vogue in the last decade or so? Bradbury got there first, but through commercial necessity rather than literary experimentation. Yet these stories do what, to my mind, only the very best sci-fi stories (or, perhaps, stories *tout court*) can do. Each one creates its own pocket universe. And their engines are, as often as not, huge ideas.

Take just one: the justly famous 'A Sound of Thunder'. Eckels, a wealthy tourist from 2055, travels back to the age of the dinosaurs on a time safari. He has arranged to shoot a T-Rex – one who was going to be squashed by a falling tree only minutes after his hunt, carefully chosen so as to minimize any chance of altering the future. And so as not to disturb the past, Eckels and his guides must keep to a special levitating path. In the course of the hunt Eckels loses his bottle and stumbles off the path into the undergrowth. On returning to his own time, he finds everyone speaking a slightly different language. He looks on the sole of his boot and finds a squashed butterfly. That titular sound of thunder, with which the story ends, is Eckels turning his gun on himself.

What would four astronauts, sent off to their dooms in different directions when their ship explodes, talk about while their communications last? What if the loneliness of deep space drove its voyagers mad? What if there was a planet where it rained ceaselessly for years, and on the one day that the sun came out, just for a couple of hours, one child had been locked in a cupboard by bullies and was forgotten until afterwards? What if the last of a race of prehistoric sea-monsters fell in love with a foghorn? What if the Messiah travelled from planet to planet? What if the crowds who appear as if from nowhere to gawp at the scenes of accidents are, somehow, *the same crowd every time*?

Those ideas weren't just intellectual. They were visceral. The story

'Skeleton', for instance, is steeped in an almost Cronenbergian body-horror. Its protagonist is a hypochondriac who is feeling aches in his bones. Having been turned away yet again by the GP who has established that there's nothing wrong with him, he consults a 'bone specialist' he finds in the directory, one M. Munigant. M. Munigant has a whistling voice and eager, shiny, darting eyes, and he alludes darkly to 'an unsympathetic co-ordination between soul, flesh, and skeleton'. Our hero becomes obsessively and horribly aware of his own skeleton.

> 'Darling, will you come meet the ladies?' His wife's clear, sweet voice called from far away. Mr Harris stood. His SKELETON held him up! This thing inside, this invader, this horror, was supporting his arms, legs, and head! It was like feeling someone just behind you who shouldn't be there. With every step, he realized how dependent he was on this other Thing.
>
> 'Darling, I'll be with you in a moment,' he called weakly . . . A moment later he stood among the ladies, being introduced to Mrs Withers, Mrs Abblematt, and Miss Kirthy, all of whom had skeletons inside them, but took it very calmly, because nature had carefully clothed the bare nudity of clavicle, tibia, and femur with breasts, thighs, calves, with coiffure and eyebrow satanic, with bee-stung lips and – LORD! shouted Mr Harris inwardly – when they talk or eat, part of their skeleton shows – their teeth! I never thought of that. 'Excuse me,' he gasped, and ran from the room only in time to drop his lunch among the petunias over the garden balustrade.

The upshot of all this is a final home visit from the mysterious M. Munigant, and the story ends with Harris's wife arriving home. On the way,

> she almost ran into this little dark man who smelled of iodine. Clarisse would have ignored him if it were not for the fact that as she passed, he took something long, white and oddly familiar

from his coat and proceeded to chew on it, as on a peppermint stick. Its end devoured, his extraordinary tongue darted within the white confection, sucking out the filling, making contented noises.

And what she finds on the living-room floor . . . My God, that one stayed with me. In another of his greatest hits, 'The Small Assassin', he takes the most sacred given about the innocence of the child and turns it on its head. What if a newborn child was absolutely determined to kill its parents? Looked at from one angle – indeed, on the face of it, for most of the story – it looks like a study in post-partum psychosis. But then the paranoid fantasy of the infant's mother turns out to be true; just as in 'Skeleton', what at first looks like a psychiatric disorder is just an inkling of a truly strange and horrible warp in reality. And, yeech, the ending!

It's telling that 'The Small Assassin' is, as are so many of his best stories one way or another (check out 'The Veldt' and 'The Playground'), rooted in childhood. Childhood fantasies and terrors and wonders fuelled Bradbury's imagination; and he knew that children are never innocent.

'Drunk – and in Charge of a Bicycle' begins with Bradbury describing getting a fan letter from, of all people, Bernard Berenson. I wrote Bradbury a fan letter, too. In the mid-noughties, as literary editor of the *Daily Telegraph*, I acquired the serial rights to a piece by Bradbury and put it on the cover of the books section. We used a rust-coloured image of the surface of Mars as an illustration.

When it was printed, I folded two copies of our section into an envelope and posted them to him. I enclosed a handwritten note saying how much his work had meant to me. It felt like sending a message in a bottle, or a rocket towards Mars. I don't know if they ever reached him. But I hope they did.

SAM LEITH is literary editor of *The Spectator*.

No Ribaldry Please, We're British

VICTORIA NEUMARK

Our family Bible came from our mum's side. But our real missals were her poetry books – *Come Hither*, edited by Walter de la Mare, and *The Golden Treasury*, edited by Francis Turner Palgrave. Now I have these same books, and they are indeed full of treasure – not least, the pleasure of remembering shared readings, with special emphasis on wordplay and on the almost sensual pleasure of drenching ourselves in emotion.

Many of the poems were the source for rhymes and phrases woven into Mum's daily speech, often accompanied by meaningful looks to underscore their importance. Sighing and shaking her head on hearing that a well-known person had died, she might remark, 'All, all are gone, the old familiar faces' (Charles Lamb, 'The Old Familiar Faces'). Or, with a curl of her lip at a history programme on TV, 'Look on my works, ye mighty, and despair' (Shelley, 'Ozymandias'). Struck by the beauty of the hilly landscape while walking across Hampstead Heath, she might refer to 'thoughts that oft do lie too deep for tears' (Wordsworth's 'Ode on Intimations of Immortality', a poem whose title she enjoyed rolling around her mouth). Seaside trips might lead her to declaim 'Break, break, break, on thy cold grey stones, O sea!' (Tennyson, 'In Memoriam'), while a big hug might conclude with 'How do I love thee? Let me count the ways' (from Elizabeth Barrett Browning's 'How Do I Love Thee?'). Naturally, she was a sucker for the Barrett-Browning love story, though I am not so sure that she was

Francis Turner Palgrave, *The Golden Treasury* (1861)
Pan Macmillan · Hb · 448pp · £10.99 · ISBN 9781509888764

au fait with Tennyson's stifled love for Arthur Hallam. That didn't matter, since 'Oh that 'twere possible/ After long grief and pain/ To feel the arms of my true love/ Round me once again' (from Tennyson's 'Maud') meant far more to her in her grief over my father's early death than the Kaddish, the Jewish prayer of remembrance.

My parents were potty about each other, though this often manifested itself in flaming rows where plates were thrown and axes hurled (yes, this did happen, though only once). Greetings might be passionate embraces or passionate reproaches. We children would squirm with embarrassment when she applied the words of Christina Rossetti's 'Birthday' to my father: 'Because the birthday of my life/ Is come, my love is come to me.' Still, this was preferable to getting all maudlin about her own mother: 'But she is in her grave, and, oh,/ The difference to me!' (Wordsworth, 'To Lucy').

We took *The Golden Treasury*'s selection of English verse for granted, but in fact its story is instructive and surprising. First published in 1861, it has claims to be the most popular anthology of English verse ever. Palgrave divided 'all the best original lyrical pieces and songs in our language – and none beside the best' into four 'books', or sections, from 1560 to 1860. It is still very popular – indeed we had it in my primary school in the 1950s.

The Golden Treasury has appeared in several editions, two of them updated by Palgrave in his lifetime (1875 and 1897). The 1897 one included a 'second series' with works by Tennyson, whom Palgrave idolized. A supplementary fifth 'book' edited by Laurence Binyon in 1926 added to the selection already expanded by Palgrave. It was this edition, containing late Victorian, Georgian and War poets as well as Palgrave's original selection, that was canonical in our household.

Palgrave had several idiosyncratic guidelines, which have been widely mocked by critics and academics, but which have struck chords with the book-buying public throughout the English-speaking world. First and foremost, he rejected the suggestion that his was 'an' anthology, a set of 'gems' or 'pearls' of English verse. No, it was 'the' anthology, containing 'all' the best lyrical poetry, so that what was left out was left out on purpose.

Turning to it now, after a long lifetime of reading, I ask myself, what was left out? The reply is – oh, so much, all of it reflecting the seriousness of the mid-Victorians. Occasional verse (too trivial for Palgrave's taste, so that even Shakespeare's songs were omitted from the first edition), satire, anything political or topical, anything mystical and not Christian, anything sexual or humorous, anything obscure or indeed anything that did not meet the criteria of unity and simplicity which Palgrave shoehorned in from Aristotle's *Poetics*. So, much of the glory of English poetry, from Chaucer to the Metaphysicals to Pope's wit and Byron's satire. No ribaldry, please, we're British. Which leads to a very odd selection of Burns and Herrick, neither of them exactly strangers to the bawdy. Yet most of what is included fits many people's definition of poetry as a thrilling fix of emotion and image to help us make sense of life.

In 1861, the time was ripe for a collection that would introduce a wider public to the riches of English literature. Other collections were fusty, musty and hard to find. The groundswell of agitation which would result in the 1870 Education Act and a largely literate public bent on self-improvement was growing. Palgrave was the man for the hour. His father was a converted Jew who set up the Public Record Office. Palgrave himself went to Balliol College, Oxford, and became one of the set clustering round its Master, Benjamin Jowett, that included the poet Arthur Hugh Clough and Tom Arnold, son of the famous Rugby headmaster.

A prodigy as a boy, Palgrave was an accomplished classicist, a minor poet and a scathing critic. He became a teacher and then a civil servant at the Education Office, and was a lifelong advocate for the teaching of English literature, even if it displaced Latin and Greek: he declared that it 'must be read much and by many' in the 'interests of a living literature'. A quality text for school use seemed to him of paramount importance.

Though a serious-minded man, he differed from other critics of the day in stressing not the morality of texts but their Beauty (with a capital B). He called the *Treasury*'s highly idiosyncratic structure 'symphonic organization' – although the 'books' are vaguely chronological, the poems in each section follow what he termed 'the most poetically effective order'. Usually this moves from Nature to love – the power of attraction, its passionate consummation, its disappointments – and then on to martial valour, death and mourning. As part of this arrangement, early editions had no index of titles, just one of first lines and poets, thus forcing readers to browse and find new 'treasure'. It is the antithesis of a Kindle.

Palgrave was not driven simply by the desire to establish the canon of lyrical poetry. He was forever trying to gain the approval of Tennyson, who found him a terrible bore and only consented to being involved in the *Treasury* to shut Palgrave up. He demanded that Gray's 'Elegy' and Milton's 'L'Allegro', 'Il Penseroso' and 'Lycidas' be included, though the last is in blank verse, which Palgrave had wanted to exclude as not lyrical enough. Tennyson, who also enjoyed reading aloud, spent an evening declaiming Palgrave's selections to his family of female acolytes, saying how much he admired Lyly's 'Cupid and My Campaspe Played' and that he would rather have written Lovelace's 'To Lucasta, Going to the Wars' than anything he himself had written. These are some of the lightest pieces in the selection, put in at Tennyson's insistence and notable for grace and charm rather than intense feeling. Perhaps they were Tennyson's answer to Palgrave's solemnity.

The Poet Laureate wrote wearily to his family about the torture of Palgrave's company. Grumpily, he refused to allow any of his poems to be used in the *Treasury* until he was dead, and Palgrave observed mournfully that including the Laureate's poems would be one miserable consolation for having 'overlived' him. Solely because of Tennyson's obduracy, Palgrave decided to include no living poets whatsoever. The unintended consequence was that over thirty years, and two editions, *The Golden Treasury* established its 'brand', as we might say today, with no real objections.

However, as soon as Tennyson died in 1897 and living poets were included, all hell broke loose. But Palgrave did not live more than a month to see this. And by this time, school libraries had already committed to buying the book.

Readers of the later editions, like my mum, were blissfully ignorant of such critical wrangles. The bowdlerization of Shakespeare, the remorseless butchery of such Tennyson works as 'In Memoriam' (a complex poem whose structure is ignored) and the omission of the final sestet from Sidney's sonnet 'My true love hath my heart' went unremarked by her and millions of others.

For Palgrave, *The Golden Treasury* was a winner in more than simply financial terms. An earlier rejection in love had led to a breakdown, leaving Palgrave with depressive, even suicidal tendencies, but after the book was published in 1871 his star rose, and in 1872 he married. He campaigned for women's education and for public access to the arts, becoming a prominent public figure while often making enemies with his vitriolic comments. He supported the Pre-Raphaelite Brotherhood and in 1885 became Oxford Professor of Poetry.

Palgrave was eccentric and unconventional, and yet his work was a vital influence in making English literature part of the national psyche. Turning back to my little green book I find:

> Only the actions of the just
> Smell sweet, and blossom in their dust.
> (Thomas Shirley, 'Death the Leveller')

Having recently retired from the jungle of higher education, VICTORIA NEUMARK is free to wander self-indulgently in the gardens of poesie.

Accentuating the Positive

ANTHONY QUINN

According to my journal I first read Molly Hughes's memoir *A London Child of the 1870s* in October 2005, 'a record of Islington life so charming and droll I'm puzzled as to why I'd not come across it before'. I might not have come across it then either had my wife not given me a copy, just reissued by Persephone Books in its appealing dove-grey livery with William Morris endpapers. It was a perfect choice for someone obsessed by Victorian London in general and Victorian Islington in particular. To my delight the author and her family had lived at No. 1 Canonbury Park North, an address about five minutes' walk from where I write this. Their house is no longer standing, though the references to Upper Street, Essex Road and Highbury New Park sound a welcoming refrain, and such is the peculiar immediacy of the writing that it takes no very great leap of imagination to see an organ-grinder on the pavement, or a child bowling a hoop, or a tram upon the Holloway Road.

'We were just an ordinary, suburban, Victorian family, undistinguished ourselves and unacquainted with distinguished people,' writes Molly in her preface. 'Ordinary' the Thomas family were, perhaps, in social and economic terms, with a father who did something in the City, a pious but fun-loving mother and five children, resident in a large (rented) house with a cook and servants. Up close, however, people become *extra*ordinary,

---

Molly Hughes, *A London Child of the 1870s* (1934)
Persephone Books · Pb · 200pp · £13 · ISBN 9781903155516

none more so than Molly, the youngest child (b. 1866) and devoted to – nearly besotted by – her four older brothers, Tom, Dym (Vivian), Charles and Barnholt.

I had forgotten from my first reading what a circumscribed life she had compared with the boys, who seem to be constantly engaged in pranks and high jinks. Whether on account of her age or her sex Molly was excluded from all trips and entertainments, never taken to 'anything more exciting than a picture gallery, not even to a pantomime at Christmas' – nor to the Tower, the Crystal Palace or Madame Tussaud's. She supposes the boys must have felt sorry for her, because when she exclaims 'How lovely it must be to go on the top of a bus!' Dym and Barney whisk her off to do just that, and there follows the most vivid account of riding atop an Islington omnibus, not on the knifeboard seat but right next to the driver, 'gently' touching his whip to the horse.

For the first eleven years of her life Molly doesn't even go to school but is home-taught by her mother, a resourceful woman whose arithmetic may have been 'at the level of the White Queen's' but who evidently inspired in her daughter a love of reading. Indeed, so steeped in literature was the family, so often did they talk of books at table that 'the Micawbers and Becky Sharp and Lamb appeared to my childish mind as some former friends of mother's, whom I recognized with delight later on when I read the books for myself'.

An irrepressible sort of joy rises from these pages, even amidst the most unpromising circumstances. The strangeness of Victorian Sundays, for instance, reveals Molly at her most amused and sceptical. Her mother insists upon their all attending a service, and not at any local church but at St Paul's itself, the family walking there 'in detachments' while their father, much less devout, beguiles the time with games of 'wayside cribbage'.

Once in the cathedral the service bores them to sobs ('sermons were seldom less than three-quarters of an hour') but what helps them endure is the 'inspiriting' music, no dreary hymns either but

No. 1 Canonbury Park North

the majestic stuff of 'Te Deums, Psalms, Creeds, Introits, and Kyries'. She and the boys knew all the chants and back at home would happily converse to their tunes. Nor were they above guffawing at Charles's impersonations of the vicar. It was hard, nonetheless, when their mother's pious observance put the kibosh on all work and play and even the reading of novels. Sunday afternoons hung heavy, but by evening their father, chafing at his wife's 'superstitious restrictions', decided that reading aloud was permissible and lifted the mood with choice bits of Shakespeare and *The Pickwick Papers* which, by some odd dispensation of her mother's conscience, did not count as a novel ('They were "papers"').

Dickens, who had died in 1870, is a strong but mostly unspoken influence here, whether in the staging of home theatricals, the starting up of their own magazine (*The Bee*) or the natural overflow of gaiety. Molly's taste for the comical and grotesque is one that the Inimitable would have admired. She makes great play of the frequent 'callers' at Canonbury Park, in particular the never-ending visits of unloved aunts, of whom 'Aunt Polly was the worst', always calling just before a meal with avowals that she 'couldn't stop' and then allowing herself to be persuaded to dine, and even to stay the night. In the general exasperation with their kinfolk one can hear Molly's private relish, honing an anecdote to a point that she will use to entertain the rest of the family after this or that caller has departed.

The exception to this disobliging company of relatives is Molly's beloved aunt Tony, whose farm in Cornwall is the site of Arcadian family holidays, though the twelve-hour journey from Paddington in a dirty, comfortless train carriage is a trial that exhausts even the Thomases' appetite for jollity. Here Molly and her swarm of cousins gambol around Tony's ancient manor-house, play on the beach and engage in more historical drama. Determined to avoid another dull visitor she and her cousin Mina perch in a tree, pretending to be Charles II and his faithful Penderel hiding from Cromwell's soldiers ('"Hark, your Majesty!" whispered Mina. "They approach!"').

One of the most remarkable aspects of this remarkable book is the distance from which its author recalls these events. *A London Child of the 1870s* was published in 1934, by which time Molly was living in retirement at Cuffley, Hertfordshire, following a career as teacher, inspector of schools and author of guidebooks and histories. Three more volumes of reminiscence – *A London Girl of the 1880s*, *A London Home of the 1890s* and *A London Family Between the Wars* – chronicled her life as a wife and mother. This long lapse of time taps into another Dickensian undercurrent, one of pathos, whose full meaning only came to my notice on reading Adam Gopnik's fine preface to the Persephone edition. The family idyll of *A London Child* ends, abruptly, in November 1879 with the news of her father's death in a road accident. In fact he had been embroiled in a financial scandal and had killed himself at a railway station – a grim echo of the disgraced schemer Ferdinand Lopez, blown to 'bloody atoms' at the Tenway Junction in Trollope's *The Prime Minister* (1876). The surface of genteel respectability on which families like the Thomases moved was thinner than we, and perhaps they, knew.

How Gopnik discovered this I'm not sure, but the revelation may prompt us to wonder at how much else Molly suppressed or transformed when she came to compose her memoirs. She had had her share of personal tragedy. Two of her brothers died young, and her daughter Bronwen, born in 1898, died a year later. Her lawyer husband, Arthur Hughes, was knocked over and killed by a tram in February 1918, a loss that sent her 'crazy with grief'. It is curious then that she recast her father's demise in the image of her husband's nearly forty years later. Was the shame of a suicide still too much to confess? Gopnik imaginatively ascribes it to Molly's search for a 'pattern', and salutes her courage in making what cannot be borne bearable: 'People who look at Molly's work as narrowly nostalgic, or imagine that she provides a view in some way "comfortable" miss the desperation of her subjects, or their real grace in the face of it.' That desperation centred largely upon money, and it is only through her passing references to the family's circumstances that we understand just how hard-pressed they were.

If Molly Hughes to some extent soft-pedalled the reality of a middle-class Victorian existence it is still much to her credit that the tone she strikes in *A London Child* is so cheerful, and so charming. She has given the age through which she lived a kindlier, friendlier aspect than it maybe deserved. It is an age that seems impossibly distant, and then suddenly very near, in particular when she remarks upon the eerie silence that reigned on Islington streets back then:

> Sometimes everything had been so quiet for so long that the sound of a passer-by or of a butcher's pony would take on a distant, unreal tone, as if it were mocking me.

Writing this on the last day of March 2020, with London inconceivably under lockdown and the roads almost empty of people and traffic, I am nearer to understanding why the quiet of a great city unnerved her.

ANTHONY QUINN's next novel, *London, Burning*, will be published in March 2021.

Scaling Gibbon's Everest

RICHARD CROCKATT

Edward Gibbon's *The History of the Decline and Fall of the Roman Empire* (published in six volumes between 1776 and 1788) must rank among the best known of unread or partly read books. At over 3,000 pages it is written in the sometimes convoluted style of the eighteenth century and lingers over details which mean little now to most readers, not least disputes over the nature of the Holy Trinity. Yet this Everest of a book asks to be scaled and in the end retirement offered me leisure and the necessary oxygen to make the attempt.

Four months of page-turning were amply rewarded, thanks to Gibbon's native wit and irony which make light work of his evidently serious theme. The opening paragraph itself entices the reader in with the author's trademark tone of amused scepticism at the foibles of human nature. At its height during the second century AD, he writes, the Empire 'comprehended the fairest part of the earth, and the most civilized portion of mankind' where the 'peaceful inhabitants enjoyed and abused the advantages of wealth and luxury' – a typical pairing ('enjoyed and abused') of contrasting terms which tell you that this author commands judgement but also detachment. Only three pages in, British readers find their own land on stage. Gibbon notes that the latest imperial acquisition was the province of Britain 'after a war of about forty years, undertaken by the most stupid [Claudius], main-

Edward Gibbon, *The History of the Decline and Fall of the Roman Empire* (6 vols., 1776–88) is out of print but we can obtain second-hand copies. There is an abridged edition available in paperback from Penguin: 848pp · £12.99 · ISBN 9780140437645.

tained by the most dissolute [Nero], and terminated by the most timid of all the emperors [Domitian]'. The Roman conquest was made easier, notes Gibbon in a remark which may apply beyond the period in question, by the behaviour of the various British tribes who 'possessed valour without conduct, and the love of freedom without the spirit of union'. Our mountain guide, though taking us over challenging ground, does so with a sense of humour.

Gibbon's vast narrative has been justly described as the bridge between the ancient and modern worlds. It tells the story of the Roman Empire from the zenith of its power in the second century AD, a moment of relative peace scarcely to be repeated, to the fall in 1453 of Constantinople, the city to which the seat of Empire had migrated a thousand years before.

Another way of describing the book is to say that it charts the emergence of the nations of Europe out of the debris of the Roman Empire. Along the way we witness relentless waves of 'barbarian' invasions, the growing political and religious split between the Eastern and Western empires, the titanic struggle of the Christianized Empire with Islam from the seventh century onwards, taking us through the crusades to the Muslim capture of Constantinople, and repeated but vain attempts along the way to restore the Empire's former glories. But this is no mere narrative. Gibbon is always the analyst or 'philosophic historian' as well as the storyteller. The reflective, ironic strain in his history, rather than its sheer length and scope, is what makes it so compelling and important.

The question which has attracted most attention ever since the work was first published is the role that Gibbon ascribes to the rise of Christianity in the decline and fall of the Roman Empire. Many early readers deplored Gibbon's religious scepticism, manifest in his frequent use of the word 'superstition' to describe religious belief of all stripes. The reaction to his history in some quarters was such that, following publication of the first volume, Gibbon wrote an eighty-page vindication of his characterization of Christianity. He was not, he said, anti-Christian, only against the abuse of Christianity.

Actually, though Gibbon undoubtedly voiced the characteristic religious scepticism of the Enlightenment, it is misleading to focus excessively on this theme in the *Decline and Fall*. 'The introduction, or at least the abuse, of Christianity, had *some* influence on the decline and fall of the Roman Empire', he wrote, largely because in the spread of Christianity 'the active virtues of society were discouraged'. In effect the Romans' capacity to fight their enemies declined while religious zeal fomented internal disorder.

Beyond the influence of Christianity, the decline of Rome, Gibbon said, was 'the natural and inevitable effect of immoderate greatness'. As the appetite for expansion exceeded its reach, the Empire struggled to control its territories. Along with this went a chronic inability to establish a stable form of imperial succession. Although at various times and in various forms heredity and election were tried, no mechanism achieved legitimacy. A few emperors lived to a ripe old age and died in their beds but an alarming number were usurped, exiled, murdered or otherwise disposed of. Becoming emperor was a high-risk venture. Instability at the top was mirrored in the wider society where civil conflict was endemic. In short, the Empire was constantly wracked by internal strife as well as external attacks.

In developing these themes what impresses in Gibbon's writing is the sheer scope of his historical imagination which ranges not only over great swathes of time but also space. It is not too much to say that in taking on the history of the Roman Empire Gibbon was taking on world history (of the then known world). Not that at any stage, even at its height, the Empire controlled everything, but even at its weakest it was a factor in the doings of other major powers. Long after it had ceased to be the dominant force, the idea of the Roman Empire retained its potency, to such an extent that hundreds of years after the capital of the Empire moved east to Constantinople the emperors and their entourage, who were mainly Greeks, persisted in describing themselves as 'Romans'.

The same aspiration to the prestige of Rome was visible in the many challengers to the Empire. With one hand they sought to destroy the Empire and with the other to emulate it. In many cases, especially up to the sack of Rome in AD 476 which ended the Western empire, Rome was able to face down its enemies through sheer military strength by means of its notorious phalanx. In other cases Rome co-opted challengers, using the armies of former enemies as mercenaries to defeat new enemies, and it also sought to neutralize challengers by buying them off. Each of these strategies had weaknesses. Outright defeat of an enemy, unless it destroyed a whole people, stoked resentments which led inevitably to renewed challenges. Co-opting foreign armies compromised or diluted the Romanness of the Empire, while buying off enemies could only be a temporary solution so long as the challengers retained the capacity to mount new attacks. Who were these challengers?

Among the earliest were various branches of Goths, who were nomadic Germanic peoples from eastern Europe, Vandals from the same region, and Huns who originated in central Asia and spread westwards from the fourth century onwards. The names of these barbarian hordes have become bywords for the destruction of civilization, yet once their nomadic existence came to an end they became a part of the fabric of the emerging civilization of Europe.

The Franks were likewise a Germanic people whose name first appears in the third century AD, occupying the area now formed by France and Germany, and who were an early thorn in the side of the Roman province of Gaul. Further afield the Romans were engaged in war with the Persians as early as the third century AD while the fearsome Scythians, distinguished as masters in the use of the horse in warfare, were renowned from ancient times 'for their invincible courage and rapid conquests'; they preyed on Roman territories in the east while the western provinces were under attack by Goths and Huns.

Following the launch of Islam in the seventh century and its rapid spread in North Africa, the Middle East and Asia, the Empire was more or less continuously embroiled in conflict with the 'Saracens', as Christians in the Middle Ages described the peoples who had adopted Islam. In the eleventh century the Normans, transplanted Norse men who lived in northern France, established a kingdom in Sicily at Rome's expense which endured in various guises till the early nineteenth century. The extraordinarily swift and destructive invasions of the Mongols from central Asia in the thirteenth century left the Roman Empire and many other powers reeling. 'Since the invasion of the Arabs in the eighth century,' Gibbon wrote, 'Europe had never been exposed to a similar calamity.' The above list offers a mere smattering of the blows received by the Roman Empire. If the story of Rome proves anything, it is that ceaseless change, often accompanied by unbridled violence, is the norm in human history.

In certain respects Edward Gibbon was an unlikely individual to embark on such a cosmopolitan undertaking. He was born in 1737 into a quintessentially English family of the middling sort. He could trace his family back to the reign of Elizabeth I when, as one biographer notes, the Gibbons were already 'prosperous Kentish yeomen'. The family had become rich through investment in the South Sea Company and were fortunate to lose very little when the bubble burst in the early eighteenth century. Gibbon's father was a poor manager of money but enough was left to provide Edward with an income for life. A voracious reader from a young age, Edward was nevertheless an undistinguished pupil at Westminster school. At 16 he was sent to Oxford where during his first year, to his father's horror, he converted to Catholicism.

In short order Edward was packed off to Lausanne, a move which was the making of him as a historian. There he lodged with a strict Calvinist charged with the task of educating Gibbon out of Catholicism, but he also schooled his pupil in classical and modern authors. Gibbon emerged after five years of disciplined learning with the ambition to pursue a literary career. He also acquired sufficient fluency in French to enable him to write his first book in that language. Indeed his Swiss education was such a success, he noted, that 'I had ceased to be an Englishman.' Balance was restored on his return home when, during the emergency of the Seven Years' War, he spent two years in the Hampshire militia, learned the rudiments of the military life and became an Englishman again. The experience, he noted, 'was not useless to the historian of the Roman Empire'.

This was a retrospective judgement. As yet there was no thought of such a project. It was on a visit to Rome in 1764, while contemplating the ruins of the Capitol, that the idea came to him of writing about the decline and fall of the city. He was peculiarly well equipped by temperament and education to undertake the project. He talked of the 'inexhaustible pleasures of study' and in the twelve years it took to produce the first volume he developed formidable knowledge of the sources which carried him through what turned out to be nearly twenty-five years of labour. Not least of Gibbon's claims to eminence was that he was a pioneer in the critical approach to historical sources.

Industriousness is expected of a historian, a quality which Gibbon possessed perhaps to a fault. At times the detail becomes excessive and interest flags, but there is a dynamism and a sparkle in his writing which reward the attentive reader. He possessed a capacious imagination which makes remote events, places and people live on the page. His portraits of the emperors Constantine and Justinian, the prophet Mohammed, Genghis Khan and countless others display a graphic awareness of different minds and cultures. In this respect Gibbon was a true child of the Enlightenment, at once English and cosmopolitan, urbanely self-confident and endlessly curious about the world, an apostle of reason and a careful and witty analyst of unreason. Gibbon's mountain is undoubtedly worth climbing for the view to be gained from the top.

RICHARD CROCKATT was Professor of American History at the University of East Anglia. He lives in north Norfolk where he sails and writes.

The Magnetism of Murder

ALASTAIR GLEGG

In 1957 I was a schoolboy in what was then known as Salisbury, Southern Rhodesia, when Arnold Jones, my English teacher, insisted that we all go with him to hear his compatriot, the Welsh author and actor Emlyn Williams, who was on tour with his one-man tribute to Dylan Thomas, *A Boy Growing Up*. This performance was a watershed in my appreciation of the spoken and written word. Williams held us spellbound for three hours: a small middle-aged, grey-haired man on a bare stage, bringing to life a child's Christmas in Wales, making us laugh at Thomas's self-portrait as a schoolboy drawing 'a wild guess below the waist', as a Young Dog with a beer bottle stuck on his finger, and then unexpectedly reducing us to pin-dropping silence with 'Do not go gentle into that good night' and 'Death shall have no dominion'. For me, this was the beginning of a lifetime's enjoyment of the work not just of Dylan Thomas but of Emlyn Williams himself.

From school I went on to the recently established University College of Rhodesia and Nyasaland, the first multiracial university in Africa, and in 1961 our Dramatic Society put on *The Corn Is Green*, Williams's very successful semi-autobiographical 1930 play about schooldays in a village in Wales. For our programme the author wrote:

> From my short but vivid glimpse of the University College and
> its setting I was able to realize how much you have the welfare

Emlyn Williams's *Beyond Belief: A Chronicle of Murder and Its Detection* (1968) and *Dr Crippen's Diary: An Invention* (1987) are both out of print but we can obtain second-hand copies.

of the underprivileged at heart, and it seems that the theme of this particular play – apart from the entertainment value I hope it will provide first and foremost! – is peculiarly suitable in the circumstances.

Ten years later I was back in Africa as a teacher at my old school, and the Welsh connection was affirmed as we introduced the next generation to what had inspired me as a schoolboy. I put on a production of *Under Milk Wood* with a cast of fifty teenagers, and stage-managed Williams's 1935 thriller *Night Must Fall*, the story of a plausible but evil young man who takes advantage of an elderly lady. What I did not realize at the time was that the play is based on a true story, the notorious case of Sidney Harry Fox, who made a living by swindling gullible women out of considerable sums of money and who was in 1930 hanged for the murder of his mother for her life insurance. Williams did not write any more plays during his long career as an actor and performer, but thirty years later he noted: 'Ever since writing *Night Must Fall*, I have wondered if a murder case would one day present itself which would challenge me to embark on a book aiming at that dual accuracy': the accuracy of both history and imaginative understanding, a concept attributed to the historian of crime, William Bolitho.

In 1965 such a case did present itself, the horrific story of Brady and Hindley and the Moors Murders. Ian Brady was born in Glasgow but was adopted by a family in Gorton, a very poor district of Manchester, where Myra Hindley also grew up. He was in trouble with the law from an early age and became fascinated by accounts of violence such as the horrors of the Nazi death camps and the works of the Marquis de Sade. Myra was originally a typical Gorton teenager. She had once dreamt of training as a children's nanny and moving to America, but instead, after leaving school at 15, she got a minor secretarial job in the same office as Brady. She was attracted to him and his perverted ideas, and over the next few years together they abducted and killed several children, afterwards burying the bodies on the moors outside Manchester, until finally they were betrayed by Myra's terrified young brother-in-law who had witnessed one of the murders.

Brady and Hindley were tried and convicted in 1966, and two years later Williams wrote *Beyond Belief*, his meticulously researched account of the case. Since then a score of other accounts have appeared, ranging in approach from the forensic to the frankly sensational, but Williams's book embodies the essence of classical tragedy, the foreseeable but inevitable descent into horror. In place of the traditional Chorus he opens with these lines from Emily Brontë:

> I dream of moor, and misty hill
> Where evening gathers, dark and chill . . .
> What have those lonely mountains worth revealing?

He acknowledges the difficulty of filling in the gap between one set of established facts and the next, and uses the term 'surmise' for his reconstruction of behaviour, conversation and thoughts to fill that gap. The result is a fascinating and very convincing eye-witness account based not just on the evidence produced at the trial, but also on his own involvement: interviews with family, friends and acquaintances of the central characters, and an artist's observation of the setting: 'the smudged evening rabbit warren of old Gorton'. The pubs, the shops, the constant but usually cheerful struggle to make ends meet, and the occasional treat: the fairground, perhaps, or the ever-present cinema. Comedy, adventure and romance of course, but also, as Williams's gleaning of contemporary newspapers shows, a never-ending parade of violence, much of it from the Hammer Films studios: 'Kings Mar 27 *The Curse of the Werewolf.* Olympia Sep 13 *Killer at Large.* Corona Gorton Oct 31 *Companions in Crime.* Essoldo Nov 5 *Wings of Death.*'

The leading characters in this tragedy are the outlaws and outcasts; Williams stresses that most of the cast are 'ordinary men and women' like Brady's one-time neighbours, the Galways, a young couple with a small baby. He worked in the foundry and was taking night classes; she sometimes sang with the local Operatic Society: 'We shall not meet the Galways, but it is good to remember that the three of them are on the other side of the wall, you can even hear them poke the fire.'

In the midst of tragedy, Williams tries to maintain a chronicler's detachment: Myra, a teenager when she first met Ian Brady, kept a diary which served as a valuable source of information, and he drily remarks, 'Professional writers apart, only virgins and generals keep diaries.' Sometimes, however, his humanity comes through: before the horrific climax there is an echo of the traditional pantomime audience's pleas of 'Look behind you!': 'Myra Hindley, do now what you nearly did. Emigrate.'

In 1987, the last year of his life, Williams wrote another book based on a famous criminal case, *Dr Crippen's Diary*, supposedly preserved until seventy-five years after the doctor's execution in 1910. Hawley Harvey Crippen was an American dentist and purveyor of quack medicines. His second wife, Cora Turner, fancied herself as a star of the musical theatre and adopted the stage name of Belle Elmore. In 1897 the couple moved to London and bought a house on Hilldrop Crescent in Holloway, an address which was to become infamous in the annals of crime. Belle constantly bullied and humiliated Crippen in front of their friends, and he fell in love with his secretary, the mouse-like Ethel Le Neve. One night, having had enough, he killed Belle and buried her body in the basement. He told friends various stories to cover her disappearance but the police were not convinced by them. In the end Crippen panicked and fled to Canada by ship, accompanied by Ethel, disguised as his young son. Shortly afterwards Belle's body was discovered, and information sent to the captain of the liner by the new miracle of wireless telegraphy. Crippen was arrested on board and brought back to England for trial.

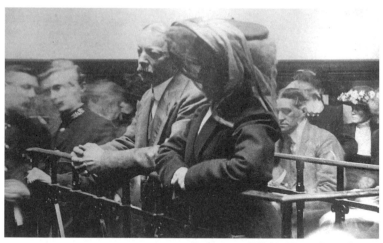

Dr Crippen and Ethel Le Neve at their trial in 1910

In the *Diary* he admits being responsible for the death of his wife but denies it was murder. The explanation he gives (which I will not reveal) was probably suggested by the line of defence Sir Edward Marshall Hall intended to pursue had he accepted the brief, according to the *Notable British Trials* account.

Williams has an ingenious solution to one of the ongoing mysteries of the case: why did Dr Crippen leave an easily identifiable item of his clothing on his wife's body when he hid her remains in the basement? The *Diary* records how the uninhibited and quarrelsome Belle mocked the prudish Crippen for what he describes as his 'quirk of keeping it [his pyjama-top] on during intimacy', and says she always called him 'Mr PT'. Years later, while burying her body he runs out of towels and goes to find something with which to clean his hands: 'What should be the first thing I fish up, but a Pyjama-Top! I had to smile . . . and looking down the hole said out loud, This is from Mr PT, and dropped it down.' It is as good an explanation as any: the police found the matching pyjama bottoms still in his bedroom drawer.

Williams brings his skill as an actor into his writing. Just as an actor must identify with the character he is portraying, so must the author of works like these somehow get to know his subjects. In the case of Crippen he is at times understanding, even almost sympathetic: 'Poor Ethel Le Neve. And poor Crippen. She loved him, he loved her. As a step towards diminishing the legend of the Monstrous Little Man, it would be fair to remember that.' Perhaps he was recalling Dylan Thomas's hen-pecked Mr Pugh, surreptitiously underlining certain passages in *Lives of the Great Poisoners*. In the case of Brady and Hindley, however, he is unequivocally outraged: their bodies may be separated by prison walls but 'their souls are together, buried on moors of their own making. And when on Judgement Day those souls are dug up, they will stink to heaven.'

I was watching an old episode of *Rumpole of the Bailey* when I last saw Emlyn Williams, then aged 78, playing the part of an arrogant elderly artist accused of the forgery of a painting which had deceived the experts. It was like meeting an old friend. He was perfectly at home on the stage of the court room, as would be expected, and clearly enjoyed the twist at the end: Rumpole gets him acquitted, but only by proving that the painting, although in fact a forgery, was actually done by his greatest rival, and imploring the jury to have pity on a poor painter 'who could not even produce a forgery of his own'. Williams obviously relished his last line on any earthly stage: 'You bastard, Rumpole, you've joined the con-o-sewers!'

ALASTAIR GLEGG lives on Vancouver Island and has retired after a lifetime in the classroom and lecture hall. He has spent the lockdown with his books; picking up the many he had put aside to read later but soon abandoning them for old favourites.

Just the Way It Is

POSY FALLOWFIELD

I first came across William Trevor in the early nineties when my son came home from school with *The Children of Dynmouth*, his GCSE set text. I've been an ardent fan ever since, although I must admit that in one's robust forties Trevor's themes (sadness, loneliness, cruelty, the sheer arbitrariness of life's awfulness) can be relished in a way that becomes increasingly difficult with age, as one's skin thins and that arbitrariness begins to bite.

One does not read William Trevor to be cheered up. But one can definitely read him to be consoled: by the pin-point accuracy of the writing, by the absolute truth of his characters, by the universality of their predicaments, by the wisdom of his perceptions – in other words, by his humanity. Yes, he seems to be saying, appalling things happen, unfair, unjustified, inexplicable, random things you wouldn't wish on your worst enemy but there it is, we're all in this together, that's just the way it is. And somehow, the beauty of the writing can turn this message into something comforting. A warm hand has stretched out and taken yours.

William Trevor was an Irishman who spent his working life in England, first in London and then, after his novels brought success, in a quiet Devon village. But Ireland and its troubles remained a favourite theme. *The Story of Lucy Gault* (2002) is set in an unspecified part of southern Ireland in a big house which has seen better days. It opens thus:

William Trevor, *The Story of Lucy Gault* (2002)
Penguin · Pb · 240pp · £8.99 · ISBN 9780141044606

Captain Everard Gault wounded the boy in the right shoulder on the night of June the twenty-first, nineteen twenty-one. Aiming above the trespassers' heads in the darkness, he fired the single shot from an upstairs window and then watched the three figures scuttling off, the wounded one assisted by his companions.

While 'scuttling' – the only emotive word in these two calm, precise sentences – may render the trespassers undignified, it also suggests something more sinister. And it is this event, typical enough at a time when houses owned by English or military families were being fired almost routinely, which reverberates through the book, affecting lives and destinies for decades to come. Lucy Gault is 8 at the start of the book; her fate, together with that of the wounded boy, is decided that night.

Lahardane, the Gaults' home, is a haven:

There was no other place [the Captain] might more happily have lived than beneath the slated roof of its three grey storeys, the stone softened by the white woodwork of the windows and the delicate fanlight above a white hall door. Flanking it on its right was the wide high archway of a cobbled yard, with cob-bled passageways leading to an apple orchard and a garden . . . a raised lawn that was separated from steeply rising woods by a curve of blue hydrangeas. The upstairs rooms at the back had a view of the sea as far as the sea's horizon.

But Lucy's parents, rattled by the trespassers and their petrol cans, eventually decide to leave and go to England. Lucy, eavesdropping, only gradually becomes aware of their decision and is both heart-broken at the prospect and angry that her parents have not explained their anxieties to her.

A solitary child, she is in the habit of secretly bathing in the sea and has also made friends with the O'Reillys' dog, 'a big, frolicsome animal,' who – while she swims – plays with her discarded clothes and hides some of them. As preparations to leave Lahardane continue, we hear of storms and fishermen lost at sea, their bodies never recovered. Lucy decides to run away, collecting scraps of food and warm clothing; but her plan to run to the house of Kitty Teresa, a housemaid recently made redundant, comes to grief when she trips in the woods and breaks her ankle.

And so it is that a false conclusion is reached. Everyone assumes Lucy has drowned, and the chance discovery on the beach of a vest and a sandal reinforces the assumption. The woods are never properly searched. Trevor coolly evokes a nightmare and we see how easily this could come about. Grief-stricken, her parents finally depart, leaving trusted servants Bridget and Henry in charge of the house and the land. By now the Gaults can hardly wait to get away but they are vague about their plans.

When Lucy is finally found by Henry and carried home she is emaciated, barely alive; her broken ankle has mended badly, leaving her with a lifelong limp. The telegram sent to her parents doesn't reach them because they have moved on.

In this agonizing way the book moves forward; Lucy grows up under the protective eyes of Bridget and Henry, and her parents continue their sad journey through Europe, eventually settling in Italy. All efforts to trace them fail. Captain Gault writes letters home but never posts them, feeling it would be an act of disloyalty to his wife, who wishes to forget Lahardane; his wife resolves to find the courage to speak to him about it, but never quite does. Lucy, meanwhile, awaits their return, badly needing their forgiveness. As she matures, wearing her mother's discarded white dresses and resembling her in both looks and speech, she is watched over not only by Bridget and Henry but also by the family solicitor and Canon Crosbie who visit her occasionally – bewildered old people who can only look on helplessly. And all the while Lahardane exerts its consoling influence.

'We hope, Bridget, we hope.'

'She has taken on the bees.'

'Bees?'

'The Captain used to have beehives in the orchard. We didn't bother with the honey the time he left. Henry can't be doing with bees, but she's started up the hives again.'

Canon Crosbie nodded. Well, that was something, he said. Bees were better than nothing.

With the introduction of Ralph, a young man who accidentally discovers Lahardane and with whom Lucy immediately feels an affinity, Trevor finds a new way to tantalize the reader. And Horahan, the boy wounded in the first chapter, reappears with a role in the story one would never have anticipated.

Throughout the book, politics rumble in the background: initially the threat by nationalists to Lahardane, then Mussolini's bellicosity which drives the Gaults from Italy, finally Ralph enlisting to fight in the second war. But Trevor is at pains to demonstrate that what really directs our lives – and certainly that of his heroine – is the humble accident. When Everard Gault, believing Lucy drowned, fears he is being punished for his military, landowning background, Trevor declares with authority, 'Chance, not wrath, had this summer ordered the fate of the Gaults.' Later Lucy rejects Ralph's proposal, insisting that she must wait for forgiveness, that 'she must trust some twist of fate – that all there was was fate'.

Events in this book, as in life, follow a painfully random course. Horahan, another of fate's casualties, visits and Lucy thinks, 'No meaning dignified his return; no order patterned, as perhaps it might have, past and present; no sense was made of anything.'

But what might seem a nihilistic stance is eventually softened as Lucy takes action in an unexpected direction; at the end there is forgiveness, peace, redemption. The past is come to terms with. As Ralph says, 'It is how things have happened . . . no one is to blame.'

This is what makes Trevor such a great novelist: he blames no one. Virtually every character in this book is gentle and decent. There are no villains. The agents of tragedy are unwitting, even witless; one of them is a dog. Bridget and Henry, protective and utterly loyal, are lovingly drawn – Bridget, pink-cheeked and excited whenever there are visitors; Henry, heavy, slow-moving, impassive. ('"More happens in a ham," Bridget's father had once said about Henry's face.') Neither of them falters for a second when it comes to Lucy's welfare.

William Trevor has been there, witnessed these things, known these people. He was surely in the room when Bridget and Henry discuss Ralph.

'He's here,' Henry said in the kitchen, and was aware when he spoke that his wife was pleased to about the same degree that he was not.

'What it is, he's teaching the Ryall boys,' Bridget said. 'She told me that this morning. He's staying in the bank.'

'So he'll go back to where he emerged from one of these days?'

'It's why she wrote a letter to him – to say come out again before he'd go.'

'He has an easy way with him.'

'Ah, he's a nice young fellow.'

'I don't know is he.'

It's not just the wonderfully odd, elliptical Irish conversations that summon character so superbly. Trevor depicts the strained, suffering parents in a sentence: 'Expert now at altering sentences already begun, or allowing them to wither or smiling them away, they gave themselves to the unfamiliarity of the place . . .' He sums up a lifetime's change in rural Ireland with perfect economy: 'Young fishermen from Kilauran with waiters' shirts on them, and cars drawn up.'

Even the dog is nailed:

The strand had been empty in both directions when she'd left it. Without being able to see clearly as she swam back to it, she knew that what seemed to be moving there now was the O'Reillys' dog chasing its own shadow on the sand.

It often did that; while she watched, it stood still for a moment, gazing out to where she was, before beginning its play again.

Who has not seen a dog daydream like that?

POSY FALLOWFIELD lives in Devon, in a village close to the one in which William Trevor lived until his death in 2016. She used to drive slowly through it, never actually spotting him but content to breathe the same air as this most brilliant writer.

Poor Show

PETER DAY

I must have bought *The Big City* soon after it was published in 1962, when Penguin was branching out from its then standard paperback format into slightly larger books with pictures, often cartoons. It cost me 4 shillings, and it is still on our shelves next to the bathroom, reserved for 'rather special' titles, to be revisited every few years with wonderment and nostalgia for a now-vanished post-war Britain.

Ronald Searle's illustrations were, of course, the initial attraction. Here they are partly St Trinian's and Molesworth, and partly extraordinary portraits reminiscent of his sketches of fellow inmates in Japanese prisoner-of-war camps. They have something of Daumier about them too. They were originally done in the 1950s, to accompany the wrenchingly poignant pieces by Alex Atkinson, which first appeared in *Punch*.

The Big City, or the New Mayhew belongs to an era just before the advent of a new wave of popular sociology, which broke in the early 1960s with the magazine *New Society* and the newspaper colour supplements. The Atkinson-Searle venture was inspired by one of the original founders of *Punch*, Henry Mayhew, whose still-famous *London Labour and the London Poor* was first issued as a periodical in 1850–2. The title page of the hardbound collected edition in four volumes, published ten years later, sums up Mayhew's considerable and original ambition: 'A Cyclopaedia of the condition and earnings of those that will work,

---

Alex Atkinson, *The Big City* (1958), illustrated by Ronald Searle, is out of print, but we can obtain second-hand copies.

those that cannot work and those that will not work'.

With two collaborators, Mayhew set down general observations about the sorts and conditions of men and women they found in London's streets, interspersed with their stories, told in their own words and condensed into an often bleak and narrow narrative. Although ostensibly humorous, Alex Atkinson's reportage has a similar tone of voice to that of Mayhew. Atkinson was a novelist, but though the stories are probably fiction, they have a ring of truth about them, which is one reason why the book lingers so fixedly in the mind.

There are only twenty-four pieces in *The Big City* compared with Mayhew's hundreds. Their titles give a sense of the modern book: 'An Income Tax Man', 'A Nobleman in Reduced Circumstances', 'A Rocking Boy', 'An Actress of Advancing Years', 'In a Night Haunt' and (particularly poignant) 'The Incumbent Who Lacked a Piano'. Atkinson's descriptions preserve the cadences of Mayhew's original detached but sympathetic prose, but the first-person testimonies are 1950s in voice and expression. Even so, these people are still as trapped in their circumstances as were the Victorian poor, still deferential to the attentive interviewer.

Henry Mayhew fleshed out in a quite remarkable documentary way the fictional lives that throng the novels of Charles Dickens. Alex Atkinson, ostensibly a funny writer for a paper whose primary purpose had always been amusement, had an extraordinary ability to evoke a fleeting period of London life when the rigidities of the interwar years were still in place but about to be radically transformed by increasing prosperity, television, relaxed attitudes to sex, and cheap travel abroad.

Chapter Ten, 'A London Eating House', is an example. The poor crowding the streets need to eat somewhere but have little money. For them, commodious eating houses have been erected 'where they might seek refuge in an atmosphere of second-hand voluptuousness' – a delicious (and typical) Atkinsonian evocation of a Lyons Corner House.

Ronald Searle

On the second floor of one such establishment, at a time of day when people might not normally be expected to be concentrating on food, the writer witnesses 'upwards of four hundred eaters, close-packed at tables so crowded that a man might easily cut a slice from his neighbour's veal-and-ham pie and stand but the smallest chance of detection'.

This London, with its street boys and coffee-house inhabitants, its street-walking Soho girls and grimy on-the-makeness, is the city actually feared, I think, by my dyed-in-the-wool provincial parents in far-off Lincolnshire. How vividly it is conjured up by Atkinson and Searle. They write and draw as if their subjects were real, and maybe they were.

Alex Atkinson has a particular talent for final lines, some worthy of the *New Yorker* master of the payoff A. J. Liebling. *The Big City* railway worker, born in Antigua, shipped into Plymouth *Windrush*-fashion, is treated as an awkward child or an amusing pet by his fellow (white) workers. After two bleak pages comes the ending: 'He was more proud to be British than anyone I ever met.'

The impoverished vicar who lacked a piano says: 'As to money, I confess I sometimes wish I could contribute to charity more freely than I do; apart from that, we manage well enough, I daresay.' That 'daresay' is almost as good as the savage modesty of the philosopher in the last lines of Jonathan Swift's *A Modest Proposal*: 'I have no children, by which I can propose to get a single penny; the youngest being nine years old, and my wife past child-bearing.'

The future of the (of course impoverished) Literary Man in *The Big City* is similarly bleak:

He told me that he would soon be forced to leave his present address, for the few guineas he earned per week did not really permit him to live (as he put it) in 'surroundings of quite such grandeur'. A friend had promised to let him have a caravan in a remote part of Kent. Here, rent-free, in a glade adjoining an orchard, with a five-minute walk to running water, he was preparing to end his days: without pride, without hope, without even the doubtful solace of bitterness.

Fittingly, the comic side of Ronald Searle is absent from most of the pictures, which dwell on the essence of Atkinson's lonely people, so that one wonders whether the picture or the text came first; the one adds to the other with ever-deepening gloom; both are indelible.

Alex Atkinson was born in Liverpool in 1916, and seems to have led an improvised life, first as an actor, then as journalist, playwright and novelist. He also collaborated with Ronald Searle on *USA for Beginners*: 'Too many books about the United States are written by men who have spent only a few weeks in the country. This one is different; it is by a man who has never been there in his life.'

But in 1960 Alex Atkinson left Britain to work in the USA as a staffer on the celebrated *Holiday* magazine in Philadelphia. He lived there at 308 South Quince Street, and there he died, suddenly, in 1962, months before my 4-shilling edition of *The Big City* was published in paperback.

PETER DAY reported on business for BBC Radio for more than forty years. He now has time to browse the shelves of books accumulated over a lifetime.

Cheers!

HENRY JEFFREYS

Sayre's Law states: 'In any dispute the intensity of feeling is inversely proportional to the value of the issues at stake.' I've noticed this in the world of booze. Some people take the question of whether a Martini should be shaken or stirred, or whether to put fruit in an Old Fashioned, very seriously. For a writer on the subject, there are two ways out of this bind: one is to take a bluff no-nonsense approach and admit that in the end it doesn't really matter. The other is to take it so seriously that it verges on but doesn't quite drop into ridiculousness. You can see the contrasting approaches in my two favourite writers on the subject, Kingsley Amis and Bernard DeVoto.

I am sure that for most readers Amis needs no introduction but I'd never heard of DeVoto before my wife gave me a small hardback called *The Hour: A Cocktail Manifesto*. I later learned that DeVoto was a historian and journalist of some repute in America. He won both the Pulitzer Prize and the National Book Award; he edited the letters of Mark Twain; and for twenty years he had a column in *Harper's Magazine*. Worthy though all this is, I cannot imagine it gave the world as much pleasure as this slim volume, first published in 1948.

The book is in four parts: a short history of American drinking, followed by the correct way to make drinks, the *wrong* way to make drinks, and an ode to the joys of the cocktail hour. Born in 1897,

---

Bernard DeVoto, *The Hour: A Cocktail Manifesto* (1948) · Tin House Books · Hb · 136pp · £10.99 · ISBN 9780982504802; Kingsley Amis, *Everyday Drinking* (1983) · Bloomsbury · Pb · 320pp · £10.99 · ISBN 9781408803837.

DeVoto would have known the old tavern culture of New York and caught the end of the golden age of the cocktail, and he would have seen both destroyed by Prohibition. He would also have frequented speakeasies and known the deep sadness of being unable to find good liquor. But when I say the first section is a history, actually it's more of a riff on history. Reading DeVoto, one has to indulge in a kind of cognitive dissonance. He both means it and doesn't mean it. The trick lies in realizing that while he is winking at you, he is also deadly serious.

Take his view on whiskey, for example: for DeVoto it is the true American spirit. It brings the country together. Whether you're a Northerner or a Southerner, Republican or Democrat, everything is better after a whiskey: 'and I'll have mine with soda but not drowned. The barb is blunted, the knife sheathed . . . in a few minutes we will see each other as we truly are, sound men, stout hearts, lovers of the true and upholders of the good.' This is the DeVoto style, soaring, heroic but with a gleam in the eye.

Better even than whiskey (rye or bourbon, not Scotch) is 'that other supreme American gift to world culture, the Martini'. His preferred ratio is 3.7 parts gin to 1 part vermouth with lemon oil expressed over the drink but no twist in it, no olives and certainly no onions, and he does not like them made in advance: 'you can no more keep a Martini in the refrigerator than you can keep a kiss there'. This is what you read DeVoto for, his pedantry and his magical prose style that always stays the right side of purple. It's like making a Dry Martini – too much gin and the magic is spoiled. A Martini should be sufficiently strong to make us believe that 'if we watch carefully, at any moment we may see the unicorn. But it would not be a Martini if we should see him.' *The Hour* is full of images like this.

Just as important as the proper way to make a cocktail are the drinks to be avoided: 'Remember that the three abominations are: (1) rum, (2) any other sweet drink, and (3) any mixed drink except one made of gin and dry vermouth in the ratio I have given.'

DeVoto abhors the kind of suburban drinkers who have a bar with a sign on it saying 'Danger: Men Drinking' and stirrers shaped like naked ladies, and who make lurid sweet cocktails from recipes found in cookbooks and household magazines. He even has names for them – Chuck and Mabel.

So yes, he's a bit of an urban snob, disdaining the provincials: 'The Martini is a city dweller, metropolitan, all cultural subtleties belong to the city . . .' But he's also wonderfully poetical about the transformative powers of alcohol: 'how fastidiously cold a second Martini is to the palate but how warm to the heart'. And he never rules out a third: 'Certainly I'll have another one . . . one more, and then with a spirit made whole again in a cleansed world, to dinner.' Doesn't an evening with DeVoto sound fun?

If DeVoto is the bard of the cocktail hour, then Kingsley Amis is the poet of the following day. You'd expect the man who wrote the famous hangover scene in *Lucky Jim* to write well about alcohol, and he doesn't disappoint. *Everyday Drinking* (1983) is made up of three collections of articles: *On Drink, Every Day Drinking* [*sic*] and *How's Your Glass?* You can safely ignore the last part which is made up of a series of quizzes but the first two are well worth your time.

In many ways, Amis is the anti-DeVoto. Indeed, he wrote the kind of magazine drinks columns that DeVoto despised. DeVoto has an American generosity about him but with Amis there's a pinched stinginess. DeVoto writes: 'if you can't serve good liquor to a lot of people, serve good liquor to a few people', but Amis says you should go for quantity rather than quality. Amis's Christmas Punch, where he tells readers to 'cut all the corners you can', sounds particularly revolting, and the Lucky Jim cocktail that he invented involves, of all things, cucumber juice. But you're not reading Amis for his advice, you're reading him because he's funny. Here, for example, is his recommendation for a boozing man's diet: 'The first, indeed the only, requirement of a diet is that it should lose you some weight *without reducing your alcohol intake by the smallest degree.*'

Inevitably, the chapter on the hangover is a highlight: 'A hangover is the result of a shock to the system, chiefly from alcohol, sure, but also from fatigue – lack of sleep, burning up energy in ridiculous and shameful activities like dancing – and thirdly from other poisons contained in tobacco.' Amis divides the hangover into two parts, the physical and the metaphysical, in which 'guilt and shame are prominent constituents'. For spiritual solace, he suggests reading P. G. Wodehouse and listening to Mozart.

If such a disparate collection of writing could be said to have a unifying theme, it's a battle against what Amis calls the 'tyranny of wine'. When he wrote these columns, Britain was at last becoming a wine-drinking country. I remember the change myself: my grandparents drank whisky and ginger ale, or brandy and soda, whereas my parents drank wine. When Amis had to write about wine, which he was often paid (very handsomely, I imagine) to do, he could never resist ridiculing the mystique surrounding it. He was particularly scathing about wine connoisseurs: 'you can call a wine red, and dry, and strong, and pleasant. After that, watch out . . .'

Perhaps the best chapter in the book is on Boozemanship: 'the art of coming out ahead when any question of drinking expertise or experience arises', inspired by Stephen Potter's *Gamesmanship*. This is Amis's tactic for dealing with a wine bore:

Wait for someone to drop a grain of knowledge, and work the old jujitsu trick of turning his strength to your advantage . . . As soon as he mentions tannin . . . shush everyone and say: 'Listen, chaps, here's a chance for us all to learn something. Carry on, Percy' – the equivalent of dropping him on his head.

When he's finished, which should be pretty soon, ask a lot of questions, the more elementary the better, like: 'does that make it good or bad?' . . . The object is to make knowing about wine seem like an accomplishment on the level of knowing about the flora and fauna of Costa Rica . . .

Amis's book is more dated than DeVoto's, perhaps because it contains contemporary references to 'Cyprus sherry' and a cocktail called Reginald Bosanquet Golden Elixir. There is, however, much in his writings of which DeVoto would have approved. Both men abhorred fruit juice in cocktails and they both championed the Martini, though Amis drank his at a whopping 15 parts gin to vermouth, and, heretically, made it in advance.

If you want serious advice on cocktails, I'd suggest you get a handbook, but if you want to enjoy two superb writers letting their hair down a bit, I'd recommend both books. Just don't take everything in them too seriously.

HENRY JEFFREYS likes his Martinis wet, five parts gin to one part vermouth, and always stirred not shaken. He hopes his new book, *The Cocktail Dictionary*, will find more than a niche market.

Daniel Macklin

These Old Bones

DAN RICHARDS

A few days before my birth my father returned from an Arctic expedition. He'd been away for several months on Svalbard – a Norwegian archipelago in the Arctic Ocean, halfway between continental Norway and the North Pole – exploring the glaciers, fjords and mountains east of Ny-Alesund, earth's most northerly civilian settlement at 78° 55′ N. It was night and raining hard when he got back. From Svalbard he'd flown down to Tromsø, then Luton, then caught several trains and finally a bus to Penclawdd, a village in south Wales. My mother, sitting by the window, saw him walking up the shining road, pack on his back. Once home he was amazed to see how pregnant she was, how round her belly.

Next morning he unpacked his bag and from deep inside the stuffed mix of wool and down he drew out a most amazing object, a polar bear pelvis he'd found on the glacier of Kongsfjorden: abstract, sculptural, bleached. A strange find from another world. I trace my love of travel to parts unknown, my interest in landscapes and the stories they hold back to that pelvis.

The polar bear bone lived in the study of our various houses throughout my childhood. It looked so pure and supernaturally white, and it was heavier than one might expect. It enthralled me; an almost feathered line of peaks ran over the sacrum and coccyx; the broken ends of the flaring hips revealed a coral interior. The hollow eyes of the femur cups, the sinuous lines of the iliac crest, its conch shell-like fissures, cracks and apertures – all these tactile features thrilled and intrigued. The idea of my father having discovered it on a glacier, in an impossibly far-flung landscape of mythical beasts, caught my imagination. To hold it was to think of my father as a young man in that great silence, tramping about in the realm of polar bears, and feel my horizons expand.

Thirty-five years on from that rainy Penclawdd night I too set off for Svalbard. I was writing a book about the human outposts to be found at the wild ends of the Earth, and the Arctic camps and cabins of my father's expedition were on my list of outliers to visit, along with a multitude of mountain bothies, desert stations, forest look-outs and sea beacons – all in light of the pelvis: totem, heirloom, embodiment of the urge for going; symbol of the fact that however far one journeys in any direction there's always history and mystery still to be discovered.

Many writers keep similar objects close by them to spur flights of fancy and creative connections. Roald Dahl had a whole table of marvellous curios beside his writing chair. A heavy silver ball of foil sweet wrappers jostled with a rock from Babylon, an opal from Australia and the orb of his own hip joint presented by the surgeon who'd replaced it.

On a similarly osteo-note, Robert Macfarlane writes in his recent book *Underland* of a whalebone owl made by the sculptor Steve Dilworth, 'a potent creation of Ice Age simplicity' which he often carried while underground 'to help me see in the dark'.

Max Porter tells me that the poet Alice Oswald has become heir to Ted Hughes's badger pelt, maybe that of the 'Beautiful, warm, secret beast' he wrote of finding on the road in 'Coming down through Somerset'. Perhaps it helped inspire Oswald's similarly brilliant brock poem 'Body': 'hard at work/ With the living shovel of himself'. The badger lives on.

The travel writer Horatio Clare, meanwhile, treasures a lump of basaltic rock from the Skeleton Coast of Namibia that is over a billion years old. Philip Hoare picks up telescopic hag stones after small hours swims in Southampton Sound, while Max Porter's writing touchstone is a piece of church pew – a half-carved foliate end, unfinished, the work paused, the craftsmen having set down their tools to go to war, never to return.

Writers' tools also take on meaning and significance – Philip Pullman recently rediscovered the green leather case containing a most important pen; a loss and return recorded on Twitter:

> Lost: a green leather pen case, containing a Montblanc ball-point pen and an ordinary pencil. I'm particularly attached to the pen, because I wrote *His Dark Materials* with it. If anyone finds it, I'd appreciate a tweet.
>
> *7:57 p.m., 25 Sept. 2018*

> Today I wore a jacket I hadn't worn for two years. In the pocket I found my green leather pen case containing the pen that wrote *His Dark Materials* . . . I knew it would come back to me.
>
> *8:10 p.m., 26 June 2019*

And while Alan Bennett, who famously writes on anything he has to hand ('I've no time for those – what are they called, Moleskine notebooks? No time for that at all'), might pooh-pooh the idea of getting hung up on stationery, many writers return to a proven combination of pens, paper and ink time after time. Repetition comforts, calms and spurs. Process manifests manuscripts.

Neil Gaiman writes his first drafts with a fountain pen – either a LAMY 2000 or a Namiki – in inks either red or blue/green. Virginia Woolf wrote in green, blue and purple, the last reserved for her letters. Lewis Carroll was also partial to purple ink and, like Woolf, wrote standing up. Like John Steinbeck, Roald Dahl began his writing day by laboriously sharpening a set of particular pencils – 'the kind with rubbers on one end. I have these sent from America by the gross, I don't know why except they are what I started with and it would worry me enormously to change the colour after 30 years.'

Alexander Dumas wrote all his fiction on blue paper, his poetry on yellow, and his articles on pink. Lawrence Norfolk, in an essay on writers' notebooks titled 'A Junkyard of the Mind', mentions that Franz Kafka wrote always in quarto-sized notebooks before trading down to octavo near the end of his life, while Jean-Jacques Rousseau would scrawl on playing cards when walking – jottings that were later written up to form *Reveries of a Solitary Walker.*

Some rubrics are more reactive than ritual. Dr Seuss kept 'an immense collection of 300 hats' to don if beset by writer's block while the musician Thom Yorke buys a ticket and gets on a train . . . day return as periapt – titfer talisman – magic bullets all.

For my part, having been to Svalbard and seen the polar bear's habitat, I feel a deeper connection with my father's adventures and the wild Arctic he encountered, so diminished in my lifetime. The trip brought home how found and fashioned objects are animated by narrative and history. None of the totems mentioned above are truly dead, archival relics. Instead, they're teachers and witnesses – prisms and provocations to further acts. There's life in the old bones yet.

DAN RICHARDS's *Outpost: A Journey to the Wild Ends of the Earth* is published by Canongate.

Bibliography

Coming attractions

LINDA LEATHERBARROW has nightmares · C. J. DRIVER enjoys a month in the country · OLIVIA POTTS jumps the queue · DEREK PARKER visits a gentleman in Moscow · PAULINE MELVILLE sees ghosts in Guyana · JIM CRUMLEY is dazzled by *Ring of Bright Water* · TIM MACKINTOSH-SMITH finds Anthony Burgess in Kuala Lumpur · YSENDA MAXTONE GRAHAM gets stuck on the mezzanine · MORAG MCINNES opens some undelivered letters · ROBIN BLAKE travels to Imperial Rome

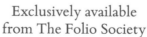